HELLO HI-LO

Other Recently Published Teacher Ideas Press Titles

More Readers Theatre for Middle School Boys: Adventures with Mythical Creatures
Ann N. Black

Multi-Grade Readers Theatre: Picture Book Authors and Illustrators
Suzanne I. Barchers and Charla R. Pfeffinger

Story Starters and Science Notebooking: Developing Student Thinking Through Literacy and Inquiry
Sandy Buczynski and Kristin Fontichiaro

Fun with Finance: Math + Literacy = Success
Written and Illustrated by Carol Peterson

Paper Action Figures of the Imagination: Clip, Color and Create
Paula Montgomery

Fairy Tales Readers Theatre
Anthony D. Fredericks

Shakespeare Kids: Performing his Plays, Speaking his Words
Carole Cox

Family Matters: Adoption and Foster Care in Children's Literature
Ruth Lyn Meese

Solving Word Problems for Life, Grades 6-8
Melony A. Brown

Abraham Lincoln and His Era: Using the American Memory Project to Teach with Primary Sources
Bobbi Ireland

Brushing Up on Grammar: An Acts of Teaching Approach
Joyce Armstrong Carroll, EdD, HLD, and Edward E. Wilson

The Comic Book Curriculum: Using Comics to Enhance Learning and Life
James Rourke

HELLO HI-LO

Readers Theatre Math

Jeff Sanders and Nancy I. Sanders

A Teacher Ideas Press Book

AN IMPRINT OF ABC-CLIO, LLC
Santa Barbara, California • Denver, Colorado • Oxford, England

Library of Congress Cataloging-in-Publication Data

Sanders, Jeff.
  Hello hi-lo : readers theatre math / Jeff Sanders and Nancy I. Sanders.
    p. cm. — (A teacher ideas press book)
  Includes bibliographical references.
  ISBN 978-1-59884-374-3 (pbk : alk. paper) — ISBN 978-1-59884-375-0 (ebook)
1. Mathematics—Study and teaching (Elementary) 2. Mathematics—Study and teaching (Secondary) 3. Readers' theater. 4. Drama in education. 5. Content area reading. 6. Oral reading. I. Sanders, Nancy I. II. Title.
QA135.6.S24   2010
372.7—dc22   2010007469

ISBN: 978-1-59884-374-3
EISBN: 978-1-59884-375-0

14 13 12 11 10   1 2 3 4 5

This book is also available on the World Wide Web as an eBook.
Visit www.abc-clio.com for details.

Libraries Unlimited
An Imprint of ABC-CLIO, LLC

ABC-CLIO, LLC
130 Cremona Drive, P.O. Box 1911
Santa Barbara, California 93116-1911

This book is printed on acid-free paper ∞
Manufactured in the United States of America

Contents

Preface

As a public school teacher for over 28 years, I (Jeff) teach language arts (as well as other subjects) and work with leveled groups of students to build essential oral reading skills. As a strong advocate for literacy, I encourage parents to read aloud daily to their children even up through and including junior high. Each year I read entire books aloud to my students, including their favorites, *Alvin's Swap Shop* by Clifford B. Hicks and *Farmer Boy* by Laura Ingalls Wilder. During the weeks that I read *Farmer Boy*, I bring the story to life by engaging students in making shoes and enjoying a feast the day before Thanksgiving, with authentic recipes from the author cooked by the students' parents.

An award-winning author, I (Nancy) have written over 300 beginning reader and leveled reader plays, mini-books, stories, and readers theatre scripts for publishers such as Scholastic Teaching Resources, Libraries Unlimited, Concordia Publishing House, and Downey Christian Schools. My best-selling book for teachers, *25 Read and Write Mini-Books That Teach Word Families* (Scholastic Teaching Resources, 2001), has sold more than 210,000 copies to date.

As a teacher/author, husband and wife team, we are dedicated to fostering a love for reading in students as well as providing tools to build essential skills in reading fluency. The intermediate level classroom (grades 4–8) is the perfect environment to continue reinforcing and building literacy skills, often even while students are learning to master cross-curricular subjects such as math, science, and history.

Using this book, students will reinforce familiarity with key math concepts while practicing oral reading skills. For instance, they'll laugh while a mad scientist learns the proper order of operations in the play "It's Alive!" and talk like pirates while discussing equations in "Talk Like a Gentleman Day." They'll learn about angles in "Super Girl" when superhero parents take their superhero daughter to the doctor because she's not as strong as she's supposed to be. Your students will learn more about positive and negative numbers by traveling to both the North and South Poles in search of the thief in "Detective Smart, Private Eye."

The scripts in this book provide the opportunity to incorporate readers theatre in a classroom of readers who are at different levels. These plays include leveled reading scripts for grades 4–8. In each script are various speakers for three different grade levels of readability: fourth grade and lower, fifth to sixth grades, and seventh to eighth grades and higher. On page ix is a chart listing the characters in each play and identifying the reading level for each character. The readability levels are defined as follows:

- Fourth-grade and lower passages: These include fourth-grade vocabulary words (or lower) as well as a fourth-grade Flesch-Kincaid Readability score (or lower). Vocabulary words are based on the fourth-grade word list in *Children's Writer's Word Book* by Alijandra Mogliner.

- Fifth to sixth grades: Although some text for these characters includes lower-grade readability, most passages of dialogue for these characters either include at least one fifth- or sixth-grade vocabulary word or have at least one sentence that scored fifth or sixth grade on the Flesch-Kincaid Readability scale. Vocabulary words are based on the fifth- and sixth-grade word lists in *Children's Writer's Word Book* by Alijandra Mogliner.

- Seventh to eighth grades and higher: Although some text for these characters includes lower-grade readability, most passages of dialogue for these characters have at least one sentence that scored seventh or eighth grade or higher on the Flesch-Kincaid Readability scale. Vocabulary words are based on Merriam Webster's *Intermediate Dictionary*.

Readers theatre is the perfect learning environment to foster oral reading skills. Paired with reinforcing key math concepts for middle grades, it doubles as an amazing opportunity for cross-curricular teaching. By incorporating leveled reading within each script, *Hello Hi-Lo: Readers Theatre Math* offers teachers the flexibility to include readers of every level in the same read-aloud play. This adds up to success for both teachers and students.

Play	4th Grade and Lower	5th to 6th Grades	7th to 8th Grades and Higher
It's Alive!	Doctor Madd Scientist Igor Creature	Townspeople Farmers	Narrator Assistant
The Royal Measurements	King Servant 2 Royal Announcers	Narrator Servant 1 Royal Scribe	Royal Mathematician Princess
Peyton's Pie Shop	Mouse Delivery Person	Narrator Peyton	Bakers King Kong
Intergalactic Treasure Hunt	Ice Cream Worker X4B4, a Robot Doomsday Aliens	Narrator Tran Tron Ryan	Princess Sasha Voices
Fraction Olympics	Announcer 1 Bobsled Pushers 1, 2 Nancy Numerator	Crowd Dawn Divider Bobsled Driver Darin Denominator	Announcer 2 Felipe Factor Bobsled Brakeman
The World Book of Amazing Records	Panda Bears Kandi the Kangaroo	Peng the Panda Kangaroos Mountain Goats	Publisher Max the Mountain Goat
Talk Like a Gentleman Day	Cabin Boy 2 Crew	Captain Jack Cabin Boy 1	First Mate
The Greatest Tug of War	Storyteller 2	Storyteller 1 Storyteller 3	Storyteller 4
A Colossal Surprise	Government Worker 2 Finance Department Worker	Postal Worker Crowd	Government Worker 1 Shipping Department Worker Builder
Detective Smart, Private Eye	Bank Teller Polar Bear 1 Big Foot	Penguins	Detective Smart Polar Bear 2
The Silly History of Transportation	Caveman Kid 1 Caveman Mom Ice Age Teen 2 Roman Soldiers	Caveman Kid 2 Ice Age Teen 1 Engineer 1 Engineer 2	Narrator Caveman Dad Roman Officer
Super Girl	Narrator Super Girl	Super Mom Neighbors	Super Dad Doctor
Out of This World Video Game	Friend 21 Narrator	Friend 3 Friend 4 Tatumn	Friend 1 Catastrophic Clones
Scavenger Hunt	Narrator Camper 1	Camper 3 Girls' Team Boys' Team	Cabin Leader Camper 2
I Spy Up in the Sky	Captain of the *Pinta* Sailor 1 Sailor 3	Sailor 2 Sailor 4	Narrator Crew

Introduction

READERS THEATRE: THE DYNAMIC DUO

Teachers everywhere are discovering the dynamic duo for building reading fluency—combining reading and drama in the classroom environment. The medium is readers theatre, and the outcome produces stronger reading skills and enthusiastic participation from even the most reluctant reader. Easily adaptable to work across the curriculum, readers theatre also helps utilize literature-based learning while studying other subjects such as math, history, science, and social studies.

If you haven't yet incorporated readers theatre into your intermediate level classroom, you'll soon discover how easy—and rewarding—using readers theatre can be. Follow the tips and suggestions in this introduction to make the most out of this book while minimizing the time and preparation it takes to assimilate this valuable learning tool into your lesson plans.

For the many teachers who already know and enjoy the benefits of using readers theatre scripts as part of the learning process, this introduction is designed to contain nuggets of gold to help your classroom experience become even better. You'll find tips, strategies, and suggestions to help you conduct successful readers theatre performances with students at varying levels of reading fluency. The goal is to provide you with the inspiration and practical tools you need to take your students on a literature-based journey to gain confidence and build important reading skills to help them progress to newfound levels of achievement and self-worth while reinforcing key math concepts.

PREPARING THE SCRIPT

Make enough copies of the script for each student or pair of students to use during practice sessions, plus a few extra sets. During the actual performance, however, the audience does not need to hold a script. This helps them observe and enjoy the performance better. If you can make only a limited number of copies, consider teaming up with another teacher and sharing scripts between your classrooms. If you have a computer with large screen capabilities, you can project the readers theatre script on the screen for students to read, thus eliminating the paper copies altogether.

INTRODUCING THE SCRIPT

As you introduce a new readers theatre script to your students, follow these steps to help them prepare to practice reading the script aloud:

- Distribute copies of the script and instruct students to read through it silently.

- Discuss the math focus of the script and relate it to the skill level you are currently teaching.

- Make a vocabulary list of the script's unfamiliar or difficult words. Have students look up the definitions, and invite volunteers to read the definitions aloud and discuss the meaning of each word.

Rehearse important drama techniques with students; these will help readers theatre come alive for those who are performing as well as for the audience. Select one line of dialogue from the script. Ask volunteers to each read the same line aloud, with a different emotion or tone of voice, such as anger, worry, fear, happiness, sorrow, excitement, boredom, shyness, weakness, or in a mean and forceful way. Discuss and demonstrate various facial expressions. Choose another line from the script and ask volunteers to read the same line aloud with different facial expressions that show various emotions. Finally, explain that body language is a powerful tool to use during readers theatre to convey emotion. Lifting the chin, turning the back to someone, pointing, or slouching are just some of the ways body language can be used during the performance. Select another line from the script and ask volunteers to read the same line aloud using different forms of body language to express various emotions.

PRACTICING THE SCRIPT

Some teachers find that a school week schedule provides the perfect framework for readers theatre. On Monday, the script is introduced to the students. Tuesday through Thursday may be used as practice days. On Friday, students perform the script.

There are a variety of ways for students to practice reading the script. Repeated opportunities for practice help students gain confidence as readers and build important reading skills as they work toward the goal of reading fluency. Whether practicing together as a class or in small groups, each repeated reading and practice session has its own benefits.

Shared reading can take many forms. When it is led by a teacher, each student follows along with his or her own script. You may pause to explain math concepts, vocabulary words, historic meaning, or unfamiliar terms. Depending on the age and reading level of your students, you may incorporate choral reading by alternating between parts you read and parts being read in unison by the entire class. You may assign groups of students to read various parts in unison. A round-robin approach can give each student the opportunity to read aloud in turn.

After students are familiar with the script, you may choose to either work on it together as a class or divide up into small groups. Each small group may practice the same script or work on different ones that you have introduced.

To assign parts to students, hold tryouts, ask for volunteers, or simply assign each role. Then allow time for students to practice reading their parts in preparation for the performance. Many students may benefit from underlining or highlighting their own parts. As they practice and participate in repeated readings, some may inadvertently memorize their parts. Because the goal of readers theatre is to practice and develop reading skills, however, don't encourage memorization. Emphasize that characters in readers theatre should always follow along with the script and read their parts aloud. This helps build reading fluency.

Some students may enjoy playing the role of director during these practice sessions. Volunteer directors may be assigned the part of the narrator to stay in the reading loop. Student directors may listen to tryouts and assign parts. Directors may lead discussions about which tone of voice, facial expressions, and body language might work best for various parts of the script. They may oversee staging, position of characters, and switching of props or simple settings between scenes. Especially with older or more advanced students, incorporating directors into the readers theatre classroom experience can offer an exciting challenge.

PERFORMING THE SCRIPT

If you choose to use costumes or props, they may be as simple or as elaborate as you wish. Following are ideas for simple accessories to add interest to the scripts.

Costumes

Readers theatre in its simplest form requires no costumes. Keeping costumes at a minimum helps maintain the focus on building better reading skills. However, some teachers and students enjoy adding simple costumes; following are some suggestions:

- Men's suit vests make it easier for the audience to identify male characters, especially if they are performed by girls.

- Scarves, gloves, hats, aprons, and costume jewelry are simple to store yet effective to wear.

- Name tags help the audience better identify the characters during the performance. Write the name of each character with permanent marker on strips of wide masking tape to wear as a name tag, or use purchased name tag stickers from an office supply store. You may also purchase a classroom set of plastic name tag badges and reuse them by having students design their own paper inserts for each new performance. A sturdy paper name tag worn as a necklace with a string of yarn also works.

Props

No props are required for a successful readers theatre, but if you choose to add simple ones, donations or thrift stores can provide used telephones, mikes from karaoke machines for announcers to pretend to use, or other items.

On with the Show!

Readers theatre scripts may be performed in as simple or as elaborate a manner as you want. All students in the script may stand or sit on stools in a row in front of the audience. The character or characters who are currently speaking can face the audience, while the others stand or sit with their backs to the audience. When it is their turn to speak, they can turn to face the audience as well. When finished, they can turn away.

If you choose to create a more formal arrangement of the characters as they interact on stage, there are simple staging suggestions for each of the scripts. Music stands provide a place for students to put their scripts as they read. A podium, stand, or desk is especially useful for the narrator or announcer, who stays in one place on the staging area during the performance. Construction paper or tag board file folders to hold the scripts lend an air of professionalism. Instruct performers to hold their folders low enough so the audience can see their faces to watch their eyes and better hear their voices. Have students practice entering and exiting the staging area if the script calls for it.

To help the audience connect with the characters and understand the performance better, it is useful to begin performances by introducing each student and the character's name he or she will be portraying.

Encourage students to read their parts with as much dramatic expression and enthusiasm as possible.

EVALUATING THE SCRIPT

After the performance, a classroom discussion to evaluate the script is helpful for students to gain a better understanding of the material. Discuss any questions about math concepts, events, or situations portrayed in the script. Compliment performers on a job well done. Talk about strengths and weaknesses of the elements of the performance, including the script itself, expressive reading, props or costumes, and staging.

For added interest, organize a readers theatre review. Students may post comments in the review to share what they liked about the performance as well as offer concrete and helpful suggestions for improvement. These reviews may be posted on a class Web site or printed out as a newsletter.

If you prefer to have a more formal evaluation of each performance, distribute evaluation forms for students to fill out. Be sure to include the author's name and title of the script and the names of each character at the top of the page. Have students evaluate the introduction, expressive reading, staging, props or costumes, and overall presentation.

WANT TO DO MORE?

To encourage students to enjoy readers theatre on their own, prepare several special backpacks to keep in the classroom. Fill each backpack with enough copies for students to perform a script together. Add simple props or costume accessories in the pockets of the backpack. Set up an area of the room as a mini-stage with stools and music stands and store the backpacks there. Invite a small group of students to visit the center if they finish classroom work early. Have them choose one backpack and practice performing the script it contains. Periodically change the scripts and accessories in the backpacks.

Script Binders

Provide binders for students to collect the various scripts they have performed. During the year, encourage small groups to switch parts and perform the script again. At the end of the year, host a readers theatre extravaganza. Invite students to perform their favorite scripts for another class or invited guests.

Impromptu Performances

Readers theatre is a great activity to incorporate into your schedule to fill in a few extra minutes. Simply keep copies of scripts on hand. When your schedule permits, distribute scripts to students and assign parts. Students may read their parts aloud from their seats or stand at the front of the room. When finished, switch parts if time permits and read the script again.

Create Your Own

One of the exciting challenges of readers theatre is to create your own scripts. At first students may feel more comfortable writing scripts based on familiar stories such as fairy tales or folktales. As they gain experience, they may create their own original scripts.

If you choose to use selections of published children's literature to create your own scripts, look for portions containing unique characters and interesting dialogue. To avoid confusion, omit unnecessary parts such as dialogue tags like "he said" or "she said." Assign the narrative portions of the text to the narrator.

Nonfiction books may be used for readers theatre scripts, too. Divide the text into small parts and assign different portions of text to different readers. Even the most straightforward expository text can benefit from the creative and dramatic reading a script provides.

CHAPTER 1

It's Alive!
(Order of Operations)

STAGING: The narrator can be seated at the front left of the stage. Seat the Creature on a stool in the center of the stage, sitting as if it's asleep. Doctor Madd Scientist can be standing to one side of the Creature. Igor and the Assistant can be standing on the other side of the Creature. The Townspeople and Farmers should wait offstage until their turn. After their turn is over, the Townspeople and Farmers may exit the stage.

CHARACTERS

Narrator	Creature
Doctor Madd Scientist	Townspeople
Assistant	Farmers
Igor	

```
                          Creature
          Assistant          X              Doctor Madd Scientist
             X                                        X
     Igor
      X



  Narrator
     X
```

It's Alive!

NARRATOR: It was a dark and stormy night in an abandoned castle at the top of a hill, looking out over a town.

DOCTOR MADD SCIENTIST: Tonight I will do the operations to complete my new experiment. Unless an accident occurs, the Creature will be finished.

IGOR: Yes. Tonight. No accident. The Creature must be finished. Yes.

ASSISTANT: Wonderful, Doctor. I am ready to help you in any way possible.

DOCTOR MADD SCIENTIST: First we will begin the operation on the Creature. The instructions say to add three legs and then six more.

ASSISTANT: But Doctor, that's not the correct order of operations. Are you sure you should operate on the legs first?

DOCTOR MADD SCIENTIST: Why does it matter what I do first?

ASSISTANT: It's of utmost importance! You must follow the rules for the order of operations. Otherwise a disaster could result.

IGOR: Yes. Rules. No accidents. Yes.

ASSISTANT: Are there any groupings in your formula?

DOCTOR MADD SCIENTIST: Groupings? What do you mean?

ASSISTANT: Do you see any parentheses in the equation you're using? Or brackets? Or braces?

DOCTOR MADD SCIENTIST: Yes. But why should I be concerned?

IGOR: Yes. Why? Yes.

ASSISTANT: Why? Because the rules state that you must perform the operations inside the parentheses or brackets or braces first. Those symbols are there to tell you which operations to do first.

IGOR: Yes. You perform the rules for the Order of Operations! Yes.

DOCTOR MADD SCIENTIST: This is my laboratory. I make the rules here. And I say that first I will operate on the Creature's legs. No more arguing! Igor, are you ready?

IGOR: Yes. Ready. This is your laboratory. Soon the Creature will be ready. Yes.

DOCTOR MADD SCIENTIST: Turn on the electricity! Pull the switch! Pump up the power!

IGOR: Yes! Yes! Yes!

ASSISTANT: The Creature! It's beginning to move!

DOCTOR MADD SCIENTIST, ASSISTANT, AND IGOR: It's alive!

ASSISTANT: Doctor, the Creature is sitting up. It's starting to speak. Oh, everything is wrong! This does not look like the Creature you were supposed to make. It has the wrong number of legs! It has the wrong number of eyes. It has the wrong number of arms.

IGOR: Yes. Everything is wrong. You did not perform the operations in the right order. Yes.

CREATURE: Where am I? Who are you?

DOCTOR MADD SCIENTIST: I am the Doctor who created you.

CREATURE: I ran away from a little old man. I ran away from a little old woman.

ASSISTANT: Halt the Creature! He's trying to run away.

IGOR: Yes. Halt! Yes.

CREATURE: And I can run away from a Doctor, I can.

ASSISTANT: Catch the Creature before he runs away.

CREATURE: Run, run, as fast as you can. You can't catch me! I'm the Strange Creature Man.

ASSISTANT: There he goes! After him! We've got to capture him before he runs down to the town.

IGOR: Yes. Capture the Creature. Yes.

DOCTOR MADD SCIENTIST: It's no use. He's already disappeared. Now what are we going to do?

NARRATOR: It is now the next morning in the abandoned castle at the top of a hill, looking out over the town.

ASSISTANT: Doctor, the people from the town are here. They want to talk with you.

TOWNSPEOPLE: Last night a hideous Creature ran through the town. Rumor has it that this Creature came from here.

DOCTOR MADD SCIENTIST: How can you be certain?

FARMERS: We saw it! We saw it run out of the castle door and flee past our farm. Our best cow went running after it, and now we have no more milk to sell.

ASSISTANT: It's all the Doctor's fault! I told him to follow the rules for the order of operations.

IGOR: Yes. The Doctor did it. Yes.

TOWNSPEOPLE: That foreign Creature ran through the streets of our town. After scaring our children, it ran through our world-renowned zoo. An octopus from the zoo climbed out of its aquarium and chased after it.

FARMERS: All the honeybees deserted our hives and chased after it. Now we have no more honey to sell.

TOWNSPEOPLE: You better fix everything by tonight, or we'll come to get you.

FARMERS: You better find our cow and our honeybees!

DOCTOR MADD
SCIENTIST: Alright! Alright! I'll take care of everything. I'll solve everyone's problems. Now go back to your town and your farms. Leave me alone!

NARRATOR: That afternoon, in the abandoned castle at the top of the hill, looking out over the town, the following took place.

DOCTOR MADD
SCIENTIST: Igor, did you look everywhere for the Creature? Did you explore the town?

IGOR: Yes. I explored everywhere. Yes.

ASSISTANT: We couldn't find the Creature anywhere. You gave him so many legs that he ran away as fast as he could. Nobody could catch him.

DOCTOR MADD
SCIENTIST: Did you find the octopus, or the cow, or the bees?

ASSISTANT: We couldn't find anything. They all must be chasing after that Creature. What are we going to do?

IGOR: Yes. What are we going to do? Yes.

DOCTOR MADD
SCIENTIST: I'll have to operate. I'll make a new Creature. But this time I'm committed to following the rules. This time I'll start with the stomach. What operation do I do first?

ASSISTANT: Are there any groupings in the equation you're using for the formula? Do you see any parentheses or brackets or braces?

DOCTOR MADD
SCIENTIST: No, not in this example. Should I proceed?

ASSISTANT: Certainly. The first thing you'll do is perform all the multiplication and division starting from left to right.

IGOR: Yes. Especially from left to right. Yes.

DOCTOR MADD
SCIENTIST: Okay, that's done. What's next?

ASSISTANT: Next you perform all the addition and subtraction starting from left to right.

**DOCTOR MADD
SCIENTIST:** All right. First I performed the multiplications and divisions from left to right. Then I started over and performed all the additions and subtractions from left to right. Now the operations are complete.

ASSISTANT: The result, Doctor?

**DOCTOR MADD
SCIENTIST:** This new Creature has four stomachs! What a tremendous accomplishment! It's almost ready.

IGOR: Yes. Tremendous. Soon the Creature will be ready. Yes.

**DOCTOR MADD
SCIENTIST:** Igor, turn on the electricity! Pull the switch! Pump up the power!

IGOR: Yes! Yes! Yes!

ASSISTANT: The Creature! It's beginning to move!

**DOCTOR MADD
SCIENTIST AND IGOR:** It's alive!

ASSISTANT: It's . . . it's a cow!

**DOCTOR MADD
SCIENTIST:** It's brilliant! The cow is for the farmer. A cow has four stomachs.

IGOR: Yes. Four stomachs. Brilliant. Yes.

**DOCTOR MADD
SCIENTIST:** Now I'll operate again. I'll proceed and make even more new creatures. This time I'll start with the eyes. What operation do I do first?

ASSISTANT: Are there any groupings in the equation you're using for this new formula? Do you see any parentheses?

**DOCTOR MADD
SCIENTIST:** Yes, and I'm anxious to know how to proceed.

ASSISTANT: The first thing you'll do is perform all the operations inside the parentheses.

IGOR: Yes. Perform all the operations inside. Yes.

DOCTOR MADD SCIENTIST: Okay, that's done. What's next?

ASSISTANT: Next you will perform the multiplication and division starting from left to right. Then finally you will perform all the addition and subtraction starting from left to right.

DOCTOR MADD SCIENTIST: All right. Now the operations are complete.

ASSISTANT: The result, Doctor?

DOCTOR MADD SCIENTIST: This new Creature has five eyes! And there are numerous Creatures. These Creatures are almost ready.

IGOR: Yes. Ready. Soon the numerous Creatures will be ready. Yes.

DOCTOR MADD SCIENTIST: Igor, turn on the electricity! Pull the switch! Pump up the power!

IGOR: Yes! Yes! Yes!

ASSISTANT: The Creatures! They're beginning to move!

DOCTOR MADD SCIENTIST AND IGOR: They're alive!

ASSISTANT: They're . . . they're bees!

DOCTOR MADD SCIENTIST: Yes! These marvelous honeybees are for the farmer. Bees have five eyes.

ASSISTANT: Doctor, they're mad! They're chasing the cow.

IGOR: Yes. Mad. Yes.

DOCTOR MADD SCIENTIST: Igor, take the cow to the farmer. The honeybees will follow. Then come back and we'll operate on the octopus. But hurry! Before the bees start to sting!

IGOR: Yes. Hurry before the bees start to sting. Yes. Ooooow!

POSSIBLE EXTENSIONS

1. Play a game of Simon Says Math. On the board, write an equation or expression students can simplify in their heads. Start the game by giving the class commands such as the following:

   - Simon says hop on one foot.

   - Stop.

   - Simon says anyone who stopped must sit down.

   - Simon says stop.

   - Simon says simplify this expression.

   - Simon says turn around once.

   - Raise your hand if you know the answer.

   - Simon says anyone who raised his or her hand must sit down.

   - Simon says raise your hand if you know the answer.

   - Etc.

   Continue the game until one person wins or you run out of time. As in a regular game of Simon Says, if students do an action but you didn't first say, "Simon Says," they are out of the game and must sit down. Be sure to give students who are sitting down chances to get back in the game so they will follow along with the math from their seats.

2. Have students each make a poster listing the rules of the order of operations. Encourage them to add illustrations or fancy letters for a better visual effect. Choose one poster and hang it in the room as a reminder of these important rules.

3. Divide students into small groups. Give each group a different example to simplify. Ask each group to work together to draw a series of pictures that illustrate how to simplify their example while performing the correct order of operations. Then invite each group to share their illustrations and explain the step-by-step process they took to simplify their problem.

4. Divide students into teams. Have each team send two members up to the board. Write an example on the board that needs to be simplified. Every team that simplifies the problem scores a point. The first team to simplify the expression scores a second point. Send those team members back to their seats and invite new members of each team up to the board for a new expression to simplify. Repeat until every student has had a turn at the board. The team with the most points wins the game.

5. Write an example on the board. Ask students to simplify the problem and complete the following paragraph with the answer:

   I am Dr. Madd Scientist. I used this formula to perform my next operation and followed the correct rules of operation. My Creature has _____ legs.

   Now have students write their own examples. (They may choose a problem from their math books if you'd like.) Instruct them to simplify their examples and use the answers to complete the paragraph above. Next have them each draw a picture of their new creatures and write a paragraph to describe them. Take time for students to share their examples, the steps they took to simplify them, and the descriptions and illustrations of their creatures.

CHAPTER 2

The Royal Measurements (Measurements)

STAGING: The royal announcers may stand at the front left of the stage. The narrator may stand at the front right. In the center of the stage, the king should be seated. Behind the king on the left should be his two servants. Behind the king on the right should be the royal scribe and the royal mathematician. The princess may wait offstage until it is her turn to speak, at which point she will walk on stage and exchange places with the king.

CHARACTERS

Narrator	Royal Scribe
King	Royal Announcers
Servants 1 and 2	Princess
Royal Mathematician	

Servant 1	Servant 2	Royal Scribe	Royal Mathematician
X	X	X	X

King
X

Royal Announcers
X X X X

Narrator
X

The Royal Measurements

NARRATOR: Once upon a time, in a kingdom long ago, there lived a king. He was a good and wise king who ruled the land with justice. One day, as he was sitting on his royal throne, he got hungry and thirsty.

KING: Servant, get me a drink of milk! And bring me a chocolate chip cookie with that, too.

SERVANT 1: Yes, your royal majesty. But first, if I may ask, how much milk do you want to drink? And how big of a cookie do you want to eat?

KING: Well, those are good questions. In fact, they are so good that I'm going to ask all of you the same thing. How much milk *should* I drink, and how big of a cookie *should* I eat?

ROYAL MATHEMATICIAN: Excuse me, sire, but we do not yet have any system of measurement anywhere in our entire kingdom. So therefore, your question does not have an answer.

SERVANT 2: We are here to serve our good and wise king, so if you like, we can help you.

ROYAL MATHEMATICIAN: Yes! We can help you invent and develop a brand new system of measurement.

SERVANT 1: Then everyone in the kingdom would use this system.

SERVANT 2: From now on, everyone would know how much milk to drink and how big of a cookie to eat.

KING: Of course! Every kingdom needs to know things like this.

ROYAL SCRIBE: I will write down everything you decide. Then I will write letters and send them out to everyone in the entire kingdom.

KING: Wonderful! Let's get started right away, after I eat my milk and cookie.

From *Hello Hi-Lo: Readers Theatre Math* by Jeff Sanders and Nancy I. Sanders. Santa Barbara, CA: Libraries Unlimited. Copyright © 2010.

SERVANT 2: And how much milk do you want to drink—

KING: Enough! Just bring me a glass of milk! That's a royal order.

ROYAL ANNOUNCERS: Hear ye! Hear ye! The royal king has just made a royal order. Bring him his milk and cookie!

NARRATOR: After the king ate his milk and cookie, all the royal servants took the king out to the courtyard. They were ready to begin measuring.

ROYAL MATHEMATICIAN: The first measurement I recommend that you invent is the measurement for length. How long do you want the standard unit for length to be?

KING: I know! I'll use my foot. It will come in handy when I need to measure something.

ROYAL MATHEMATICIAN: But sire, are you sure you should use your foot? That's such a strange unit of measurement. May I suggest you use something such as a ruler or stick?

KING: I like my foot! If I want to use my foot, I'll use my foot. After all, I'm the king! It's official. Everyone in the kingdom will now use my foot to measure length. That's an order.

ROYAL ANNOUNCERS: Hear ye! Hear ye! The royal king has just made a royal order. One foot is a measurement for length.

ROYAL SCRIBE: I'll be sure to write this down so I can send this important news out to the entire kingdom.

ROYAL MATHEMATICIAN: But sire, this poses another serious problem. Your foot is so large. What do you recommend we use to measure smaller items such as a cookie?

NARRATOR: Unfortunately, the king did not hear the question. He was busy looking at some sort of green worm that was crawling over his foot.

ROYAL MATHEMATICIAN: Your royal majesty, I just asked you a question of utmost importance. What will we use for smaller measurements?

KING:	Why, we'll use this green inchworm, of course! What an interesting creature! He just walked over my foot. And look! He's exactly the length of my thumb.
SERVANT 2:	I watched the inchworm the whole time. He inched along from end to end a total of 12 times.
SERVANT 1:	I suggest we call this measurement an inch in honor of this green inchworm.
ROYAL SCRIBE:	Perfect! I'll write down that 12 inches is the equivalent of one foot.
NARRATOR:	Just then, the royal robe makers waltzed into the courtyard. Their arms were full of yard goods—red fabric as soft as velvet.
SERVANT 1:	Excuse me, your royal majesty. It's time for your appointment to get a new robe made for your royal shoulders.
SERVANT 2:	How long do you want your robe to be? Do you like a shorter robe or a longer robe best? It helps if we know the exact measurement to cut these yard goods.
KING:	I like a long robe. It makes me look more important, and I like to look important. But if I ask for the length in inches, that's a lot of inches. It would even be a lot of feet.
ROYAL MATHEMATICIAN:	May I suggest that you invent another new unit of measurement that is longer than an inch and longer than a foot?
KING:	Of course! Since these are yard goods, I'll call this new measurement a yard. Look! I'll hold one end of fabric up to my nose and the other end out in my hand. That's a good way to measure fabric for my new robe. I'll call this length a yard. And look! Isn't this funny? One yard is the same length as three of my feet.
ROYAL MATHEMATICIAN:	But sire! This is ridiculous! We simply cannot base an entire system of measurement on things like your foot or your thumb or the distance from your nose to your fingertips.

KING: Of course we can! I'm the king! It's official. One yard is equivalent to three feet. That's an order.

ROYAL ANNOUNCERS: Hear ye! Hear ye! The royal king has just made a royal order. One yard is equal to three feet.

ROYAL SCRIBE: I'll write all this down and send these new measurements out to everyone in the kingdom.

NARRATOR: The king even made a new measurement. It equaled 5,280 feet. He called it a mile. It was the number of steps he took to carry his new baby, Prince Mile, before bedtime. From then on, everyone used inches, feet, yards, and miles to measure length. Everyone in the kingdom was happy.

ROYAL MATHEMATICIAN: I'm not happy! I think it's silly to use things like a foot for measurement. What's mathematical about a foot?

NARRATOR: Well, almost everyone in the kingdom was happy. The king even invented pints, quarts, and gallons so his servants could measure his milk. He also invented ounces, pounds, and tons to measure weight.

ROYAL MATHEMATICIAN: And was the king ever sorry he invented a system to measure weight! He put on so much weight from eating all the milk and cookies that he eventually threw away his bathroom scales.

NARRATOR: Many years went by. The king was replaced with a new king, who was replaced one day by a princess. One day the princess was sitting on her throne. She was listening to her MP3 player when she got hungry and thirsty.

PRINCESS: Servant, would you please get me a fresh drink of milk and a delicious chocolate chip cookie?

SERVANT 2: Yes, your royal majesty. But first, if I may ask, how much milk do you want to drink? Would you like one pint or one quart of milk?

SERVANT 1: And how big of a cookie do you want to eat? Would you like one that is two inches in diameter or one that is five inches in diameter?

ROYAL MATHEMATICIAN:	Excuse me, your royal princess, but may I make a suggestion? Since you're new on the throne, don't you think it's about time for our kingdom to have a better standard of measurement? We need one that is easier and more efficient for the people to use.
PRINCESS:	What a great idea! This sounds like so much fun. I excelled in math in school and would love to create a new standard of measurement that is mathematically sound.
ROYAL MATHEMATICIAN:	Wonderful! Wonderful! Let's get started right away. Immediately after you eat your milk and cookie, of course.
ROYAL SCRIBE:	I will write down everything you decide. Then I will write letters and send them out to everyone in the entire kingdom.
PRINCESS:	Eeeek! There's a bug crawling up the wire on my royal earphones, and it looks like it has 100 legs. Somebody help! Get it off! Eeeek!
SERVANT 2:	I'll help, your royal majesty. There! I picked up that scary insect here on this stick. Now, what do you want me to do with it?
PRINCESS:	Let me look at it. Oh, I see what it is. It's a centipede, and it's wiggling, and it's scary, and it really does have 100 legs.
ROYAL MATHEMATICIAN:	May I suggest we get started immediately with the brand new system of measurement?
PRINCESS:	Of course! This centipede gave me a great idea. It's the perfect length for one small unit of measurement. I'll call that unit a centimeter in honor of the centipede that gave me the idea.
ROYAL MATHEMATICIAN:	This is ridiculous! You can't create a system of measurement based on a bug. Why don't you use something mathematical?

SERVANT 1: Look! The bug is crawling very steadily from end to end along that stick.

PRINCESS: I see. We can use this stick, too! We'll call it a meter. It's as long as 100 centimeters.

ROYAL MATHEMATICIAN: At least using divisions of hundreds and tens is very mathematical.

PRINCESS: I'm glad you approve. Therefore, I officially decree that our new system of measurement is metric. That's an order.

ROYAL ANNOUNCERS: Hear ye! Hear ye! The royal princess has just made a royal order. From now on the entire kingdom will be using meters.

ROYAL SCRIBE: I'll write this all down and send out the news right away. Everyone must know about this important change.

NARRATOR: The Princess went on to use millimeters and kilometers for length. She chose liters to measure her milk and grams to measure mass.

ROYAL MATHEMATICIAN: Even I'm happy! Metrics are so much easier to use when adding, subtracting, multiplying, and dividing. Everything is a multiple of 10.

NARRATOR: From then on, the entire kingdom lived happily ever after.

POSSIBLE EXTENSIONS

1. Hold an old-fashioned spelling bee with an emphasis on measurement and math. Divide students into two teams. Take turns between teams, progressing from student to student. Give students a variety of instructions such as the following:

    – Spell vocabulary words related to measurement such as kilometer, metric, quart, pint, and pound.

    – Spell abbreviations for words such as ounce and pound.

    – Define quantities of measurement such as, "How many feet are in one mile?"

    – Do mental math problems according to the skill level you are studying about measurement.

2. Have students estimate and then measure about a dozen items in the classroom. First, instruct students to look around the classroom and locate one item that they estimate is one inch long. Then have them look for one item that they estimate is two inches long, then one that is three inches long, and so forth. Have them write down the name of the items along with the estimated measurements.

    When finished, have pairs of students measure all the items on their lists. The partner whose item's actual length was the closest to each estimated length scores one point. If there is a tie, both partners score a point. The partner with the most points wins the game.

3. Invite students to describe in their journals how they would measure the following quantities:

    – The weight of an elephant, the weight of a dog, and the weight of a feather.

    – The distance to the moon, the length of the transcontinental railroad, and the height of a favorite celebrity.

    – The amount of water in the Atlantic Ocean, the amount of milk in a cup, and the amount of liquid in one drop of dew.

    Instruct students to explain whether they would use standard measurements or metric. Have them list which units of measurement they would use and describe how they would attempt to measure each item. Their answers may be real or imaginary measures.

4. Have students measure their shoe sizes in either inches or centimeters. According to the skill level and ability of your students, have them calculate the following measurements based on their shoe sizes as the standard units of length:

    – How long would one inch be? ($\frac{1}{12}$ of the shoe size)

    – How long would one centimeter be? ($\frac{1}{10}$ of the shoe size)

    – How long would 1 yard be? (three times the shoe size)

    Instruct students to make paper or tagboard rulers the same size as their shoe lengths. They should divide the rulers into 10 equal segments on one side to represent metric and into 12 equal segments on the other side to represent inches and feet. Then ask them to use their rulers to measure various objects in the classroom. Discuss and compare results.

5. Take a survey among your students to see which prefer using standard measurements, which prefer metric, and which have no preference. Graph the results on a Venn diagram. Next to the diagram list the reasons the students gave for their preferences.

CHAPTER 3

Peyton's Pie Shop (Circles)

STAGING: Seat the narrator at the front left of the stage. Peyton may be seated in the front center of the stage, with the bakers on either side of him. The mouse, delivery person, and King Kong should wait offstage. They may enter and exit the stage during their turns.

CHARACTERS

Narrator	Mouse
Peyton	Delivery Person
Bakers	King Kong

```
            Bakers          Peyton          Bakers
     X    X    X    X         X        X    X    X    X




  Narrator
     X
```

Peyton's Pie Shop

NARRATOR: One morning, the local bakeshop was getting ready for the day.

PEYTON: Good morning! Are all of you ready for another great day of baking delicious pies and cakes?

BAKERS: Business has been really slow lately, and we haven't seen many customers at all. Do you think we'll get many orders for pies or cakes today?

PEYTON: I certainly hope we will!

BAKERS: We have a new recipe for butterscotch cream cheesecake that we'd like to make for the very first time. Should we give it a try today?

PEYTON: Yes! I just know this will be a great day for business. Mother's Day is coming. Everyone likes to eat pies and cakes for holidays.

NARRATOR: Just then the very first customer of the day walked quickly into the shop. It was a little mouse.

MOUSE: Do you make pies or cakes?

PEYTON: Of course we do! This is Peyton's Pie Shop. Would you like to place an order right away for one of our delicious pies or cakes?

MOUSE: Yes, I'd like to order something for my mother.

BAKERS: We have a new recipe for butterscotch cream cheesecake. Would you like to order it for your mother?

MOUSE: Certainly! She likes anything with cheese.

BAKERS: Do you think a seven-inch pie will be big enough, or do you want to place an order for a nine-inch pie?

MOUSE: Are you kidding? My mother could never eat something that huge, even made out of cheese. She's a mouse, not a rat.

PEYTON: Just precisely how big do you need?

MOUSE: I think something with a half-inch radius should be perfect. Can you deliver it?

PEYTON: Of course we can! We'll deliver it to your neighborhood in about one hour.

NARRATOR: The mouse left for home, but the bakers were quite upset with the owner of Peyton's Pie Shop.

BAKERS: Why did you tell that customer that we could make it with a half-inch radius? We've never made a pie or cake that little before, and we don't even have any pie pans that size.

PEYTON: Business has been so bad lately we better take any order we get. Can't you find something to use for a pie pan that size?

BAKERS: It will have to be something that has a circle with a one-inch diameter. Do you think a thimble would work?

PEYTON: It's worth a try.

NARRATOR: The bakers got to work. They made a tiny cheesecake inside a thimble. Soon it was ready to deliver to the mouse.

DELIVERY PERSON: I'll ride my bike over and deliver it. It's so small, however, I'm afraid I might lose it.

PEYTON: Whatever you do, don't lose it because it's the only order we've had all day.

DELIVERY PERSON: I'll be careful. I'll carry it in my pocket and zip my pocket shut.

NARRATOR: After he left, the next customer arrived. It was King Kong!

KING KONG: I'm looking for a place that bakes pies, and I'm in a hurry.

PEYTON: Yes, of course we bake pies. This is Peyton's Pie Shop.

KING KONG: I need a pie today, and I need it big. It's for my mother on Mother's Day, and her favorite dessert is blueberry pie.

PEYTON: Just exactly how big of a blueberry pie did you want to order?

KING KONG: Let me see. I'm having a surprise party for her, and it's going to be so big that even all the big movie stars will be there, too. I'm having it at the top of the Empire State Building.

BAKERS: Do you think a seven-inch pie will be big enough, or do you want to place an order for a nine-inch pie?

KING KONG: Are you kidding me or what? I'm talking big! As an extra surprise, I'm having a helicopter fly it to the top of the Empire State Building. I'll do anything to make Mom happy.

BAKERS: If seven inches or nine inches are both too small, what kind of diameter do you think this pie should have?

KING KONG: It should have a diameter of at least 100 inches straight across the middle. I'm talking big!

PEYTON: We'll make it happen! You can count on us to get the job done and deliver the exact size of pie that you want.

KING KONG: You wouldn't happen to know anyone who's an expert pilot and knows how to fly a helicopter, do you?

PEYTON: I could ask our delivery person.

KING KONG: That will do just fine. I'll put in an order for a helicopter to be sent over here in about an hour.

NARRATOR: King Kong paid his money and left. Now the bakers were even more upset with the shop owner than they were the first time.

BAKERS: How do you expect us to make a pie that humongous? Where will we get pie pans that gigantic? Where will we bake it? No oven is that big!

PEYTON: I know, but look at the big order he just made. Look at the big tip he just paid us. With this big money, we can pay all our bills. Just do whatever it takes to make this giant his giant blueberry pie.

BAKERS: But he said he wants the pie for his mother to be 100 inches in diameter. That's a big circle.

PEYTON: I know. I've never heard of a pie pan in the whole entire world that's this big of a circle.

BAKERS:	We've got an idea. We can make our own pie pan out of aluminum foil, and then we can bake it out on top of the parking lot. That blacktop gets pretty hot out there.
PEYTON:	I had confidence that all of you could handle a great big order like this one!
NARRATOR:	Just then the delivery person came back.
DELIVERY PERSON:	The mouse really likes the pie you made for him. He thinks his mother will be very happy.
PEYTON:	Great! But now we have another mother to make happy, and this isn't a mouse.
DELIVERY PERSON:	Who wants our shop to bake a pie this time?
PEYTON:	King Kong! He wants a pie so big it takes a helicopter to deliver it.
DELIVERY PERSON:	Who's going to fly the helicopter?
PEYTON:	You are.
DELIVERY PERSON:	I am? I've never done that before! I've never even driven a car. All I know how to do is ride a bike.
PEYTON:	Don't worry about it. You'll do just fine. Besides, flying a helicopter can't be that hard.
DELIVERY PERSON:	I'll give it a try if you really think I can do it. But how are you going to make a pie that big? Where will you get a pie pan that big?
BAKERS:	We have aluminum foil, and we're planning on using it to make a pie pan in the parking lot. What should we do first?
PEYTON:	First, grab a piece of chalk and use it to mark a point in the middle of the parking lot. That will be the center of the circle.
BAKERS:	Great. Do you want us to measure the radius next? It will go from the point in the center out to the edge of the circle itself. The radius is half of the diameter.
PEYTON:	That sounds good. Half of 100 inches is 50 inches. Measure 50 inches from the center to the edge of the circle.

DELIVERY PERSON: Can I help? I can draw a giant circle with the piece of chalk.

PEYTON: Make sure all the points on the circle will be the same distance away from the center.

DELIVERY PERSON: Done! Here's the giant circle. Now you can spread out the foil and make the giant pie pan.

NARRATOR: The bakers used boxes and boxes of foil to make the pie pan. Then they ordered enough blueberries to fill up the pan. It took *a lot* of blueberries, but finally the pie was ready to go.

PEYTON: Look! Here comes the helicopter! Stand back, everyone, so nobody gets hurt.

NARRATOR: A big truck drove up to the parking lot carrying a helicopter.

PEYTON: Okay, it's ready to go! I attached chains to the pie so it can be lifted up and carried away.

DELIVERY PERSON: Should I get in now and fly the helicopter?

BAKERS: Yes, but be careful on the way with your special delivery! Fly slowly enough so that the blueberries don't spill out over the side.

NARRATOR: The helicopter flew slowly up into the sky. Hanging from the bottom was a huge blueberry pie. Slowly, slowly, it flew all the way to the Empire State Building. There were King Kong, King Kong's mother, and all their party guests.

KING KONG: Careful! Careful! Fly that helicopter up close to the top of the Empire State Building so I can reach out and get the pie.

DELIVERY PERSON: Help! How do I stop this thing? This didn't come with an instruction manual. I can't figure out which button to push to make it stop!

KING KONG: What are you doing? You're flying dangerously close to the Empire State Building. Stop! Stop!

DELIVERY PERSON: I don't know how to stop! Watch out! I think the helicopter's going to crash!

NARRATOR: Yes, you guessed it. The helicopter crashed into the top of the Empire State Building. The blueberry pie spilled. King Kong turned blue. His mother turned blue. Everyone at the party turned blue. Even the Empire State Building turned blue. The delivery person felt horrible, but he didn't know what to do. So he walked back to Peyton's Pie Shop.

PEYTON: What happened to you? From head to foot, you're completely and totally blue!

DELIVERY PERSON: Do you want me to start by telling you the good news first, or the bad news?

PEYTON: You better give me the bad news first, but I'm almost positive I know what it is. You had an accident, didn't you?

DELIVERY PERSON: Yes, I crashed into the Empire State Building.

BAKERS: You ruined our beautiful, delicious, gigantic blueberry pie, didn't you?

DELIVERY PERSON: Yes. It spilled over *everything*.

PEYTON: Well, if that's the bad news, how can there be any good news?

DELIVERY PERSON: King Kong said it would make a great movie. In fact, he asked his mother to be the star. She's so happy she gave us another big tip. She wanted to pay us even more money than we got before.

NARRATOR: Just then there was a knock at the door. Outside stood 200 mice.

PEYTON: May I help you?

MOUSE: Can you make me some more butterscotch cream cheesecakes? Now all my aunts and uncles and cousins want one.

BAKERS: Do you think a seven-inch pie pan will be big enough, or do you want to place an order for a nine-inch one?

MOUSE: Are you kidding? We're a family of mice, not rats. We want them each to have a half-inch radius, just like before.

PEYTON: Of course! When do you want it delivered?

MOUSE:	It? We don't just want one. We want one for each of us. We want to order a total of 200!
PEYTON:	You got it. We'll deliver all 200 to you in about one hour.
NARRATOR:	The mice left, but the bakers were upset. Even the delivery person was upset.
BAKERS:	Where will we find enough one-inch thimbles to make all those cheesecakes?
PEYTON:	Business is business. We need to take all the orders we can get. Just look around. I'm confident that you'll find them.
DELIVERY PERSON:	But how will I deliver all of them? I can't fit all of them in my pocket.
PEYTON:	I guess you'll just have to learn how to fly that helicopter.

POSSIBLE EXTENSIONS

1. Ask students to write an acrostic or two about circles. They may use words such as circle, radius, diameter, center, or chord as the base for the acrostic. An acrostic is a type of poem in which the main word is written in a vertical line, starting with the first letter of the word on the first line at the top of the page and ending with the last letter of the word on the bottom line of the poem. Then each line of the poem either begins with the letter of the key word or uses that letter within the line. The lines of an acrostic poem do not have to rhyme. Each line of the poem may be either a word, phrase, or sentence about circles.

2. Play a match game to find the matching circles. Prepare for the game by drawing and labeling sets of matching circles on blank index cards. For instance, on one card draw a circle, mark its diameter, and label it as 100 inches. Draw a circle on a second index card, mark its radius, and label it as 50 inches. Draw and label sets of matching circles according to the skill level that your students are learning.

   To play the game, students place all cards individually face down. They take turns turning over two cards at a time. If the cards do not match, they should be turned face down again. If the cards reveal a match, that player takes the match and gets another turn.

   The player with the most matches at the end wins the game.

3. For this journal activity, ask students to each choose one movie monster or fairy tale character who wants to buy a pie for his mother on Mother's Day. Instruct students to draw in their journals the size of pie that character wants to buy and label its diameter and radius (or other skill you are teaching). When they are finished, have students choose the flavor that pie would be and write a short story about the character giving the pie as a surprise on Mother's Day.

4. For more activities exploring circles, visit these Web sites:

   – www.education.com/activity/article/Circumference_Radius_middle/
   – timiddlegrades.com/activitiesmath/505/
   – www.ciese.org/curriculum/noonday/index.html
   – www.beaconlearningcenter.com/Lessons/839.htm

CHAPTER 4

Intergalactic Treasure Hunt (Solid Figures)

STAGING: Have the first four characters—Ice Cream Worker, Tran, Tron, and Ryan—stand in a group at the center of the stage. The narrator may stand at the front right of the stage. Seat the Doomsday Aliens in a group on the left of the stage. Seat the Voices in a group on the right of the stage. Princess Sasha and X4B4 may wait offstage until their turns to speak.

CHARACTERS

Ice Cream Worker	Princess Sasha
Tran	X4B4, a Robot
Tron	Doomsday Aliens
Ryan	Voices
Narrator	

```
Doomsday Aliens                                      Voices
X      X      X                                    X  X  X  X
    X      X


        Ice Cream
         Worker        Tran   Tron   Ryan          Narrator
           X             X      X      X               X
```

Intergalactic Treasure Hunt

Scene 1: Planet Earth in the Year 3456, Inside an Ice Cream Shop

TRAN: If you're not busy, I'd like a chocolate ice cream cone today.

TRON: Me, too!

ICE CREAM WORKER: Here you are. Two ice cream cones. That's two dollars. Who's next?

RYAN: A double pistachio with butterscotch on top, please. It's my favorite!

NARRATOR: All of a sudden, the door swung open, and a stranger ran into the shop.

PRINCESS SASHA: Help me! The evil Doomsday Aliens have launched a secret mission to steal my fortune that once belonged to my father, King Reginald, but now is mine. Hurry! I must get it before they find it!

RYAN: This sounds absurd. What are you talking about?

PRINCESS SASHA: There's no time to explain, but if you come to my spaceship, I'll tell you everything. The gold and jewels are worth millions of dollars, so if you help save them, I'll give you each a share.

TRAN: Gold and jewels? Count me in!

TRON: Access to millions of treasure? Let's go!

RYAN: What about my double pistachio?

PRINCESS SASHA: No time for that. Come on!

NARRATOR: Before another second went by, Tran, Tron, and Ryan followed Princess Sasha. They ran up a ramp and into a silver spaceship shaped like a sphere. With a loud roar, the spaceship blasted off into outer space.

RYAN: Okay, princess, now we're adrift in space, so tell us everything. It better be worth it. I don't give up a double pistachio ice cream cone just for anything.

PRINCESS SASHA: My father, King Reginald, owned the universe's greatest riches, so he hid them safely away until I was old enough to become princess of my own planet. Yesterday, on my birthday, he gave me Planet AU79 as a gift and told me it was time to collect the treasure. But just after I found out the news, I got a terrible message from the Doomsday Aliens.

TRAN: Doomsday Aliens? They sound creepy.

TRON: Yeah. Aggressive monsters are scary!

PRINCESS SASHA: X4B4, turn on the Repetitive Memory Plasma Screen, and play the message back for my new acquaintances to hear.

X4B4: That's me. Ordinary robot. Nobody important. I just do what I'm told.

NARRATOR: In spite of his complaining, X4B4 turned on a switch, lights blinked on, and a large wall turned into a giant computer screen. Huge, ugly creatures filled the screen.

DOOMSDAY ALIENS: The treasure is almost ours. We have the keys! We've set in motion a secret plan to capture the countless riches. Soon it will be ours, and then we'll be the rulers of Planet AU79. After that, we will take over the universe. No one can stop us now. Ha, ha, ha, ha, ha!

NARRATOR: After that, X4B4 turned off the switch, the computer screen went blank, and the lights stopped blinking. An awkward silence filled the air.

TRAN: This is the worst news of the century. And these aliens look abominable.

TRON: You said it! These guys look like they could blast an asteroid into cookie crumbs.

PRINCESS SASHA: I'm not exactly sure how, but the Doomsday Aliens duplicated the keys necessary to find the treasure. It appears they have a complete set of them, but I have a set, too. X4B4, get the keys.

X4B4: There we go again. Another ordinary job for ordinary little me.

NARRATOR: While everyone crowded close to see, the robot got a box and put it down on a shelf.

RYAN: These aren't keys! If you ask me, they look just like a bunch of solid shapes made out of wood.

TRAN: That's right. Look! Here's a cylinder. And here's a cone.

TRON: There's a cube and another rectangular prism in here, too.

PRINCESS SASHA: Correction. These *are* keys. Each solid shape will open a portal that we have to time travel through to get to the next phase of our search for the treasure. My father devised a very complex system to prevent robbers from stealing the treasure, but the most complicated thing of all is that we have to follow the clues very carefully to determine which is the right key for the right portal. Then we have to touch the portal with the key.

RYAN: What happens if we make a mistake? Will we be attacked by vicious aliens or what?

PRINCESS SASHA: We will be sucked immediately into an uncharted world of vast and dreadful design where the consequences could be deadly.

NARRATOR: Just then the spaceship landed. Everyone headed outside.

PRINCESS SASHA: X4B4, bring the box with the keys. Hurry!

X4B4: There we go again. Everyone gets to do something exciting except for me.

RYAN: Look! There are two giant portals here, so how can we know which one is the right one to go through?

NARRATOR: Just then, as if out of nowhere, they heard invisible voices speaking.

VOICES: Two parallel congruent faces.
Two parallel congruent bases.
Different sides have different heights.
Make sure you choose the one that's right.
The shape of the portal matches its key.
Put the key where it should be.

TRAN: I think they're talking about a rectangular prism!

TRON: That sounds accurate. Look, here's a cube. This could be the key.

RYAN:	Wait! The voices said, "Different sides have different heights." All the faces on a cube are squares. No, it's the other rectangular prism. It's the one with unequal sides.
PRINCESS SASHA:	You're right. Look at the portals. One looks just like a rectangle. The other is a solid shape like a rectangular prism. Pick up the rectangular prism with unequal sides and touch the matching portal with it.
NARRATOR:	Ryan touched the portal with the key. Suddenly, lightning flashed! With a loud roar, the portal opened up and a new galaxy appeared in front of them.
PRINCESS SASHA:	Back to the spaceship, everyone!
RYAN:	I wish I could buy an ice cream cone at the next stop.
NARRATOR:	Everyone hurried up the ramp and into the spaceship. As they flew through the portal, the giant computer screen turned on.
DOOMSDAY ALIENS:	Too bad for you and your friends, Princess! We got through the first portal before you did. We'll find the second portal before you do, too. Soon, the treasure will be ours. You can't stop us now. Ha, ha, ha, ha, ha!
PRINCESS SASHA:	This is outrageous! We've got to hurry.
TRAN:	I just felt the spaceship land, so we must have flown at maximum speed to get here this fast.
TRON:	Come on, everyone. If we hurry through this next portal, we'll get that treasure before those alien dudes do.
PRINCESS SASHA:	Bring the box, X4B4, with the keys.
X4B4:	That's right. Just call on ordinary me to do all the boring work.
NARRATOR:	Everyone headed outside the spaceship, and they stopped in front of two huge portals.
VOICES:	Beware! If you choose the wrong key, you will be lost inside the magnetic pull of a black hole for eternity. Choose wisely, companions of the royal daughter. This key has a base that's square. Its four congruent faces rise up to form a vertex at the top. Use it to open the portal that is shaped like a cube.

TRAN: Here's the right key! It's the logical choice, so I'll use this one.

TRON: You're incredible! Go for it, buddy. The cube is the portal on the left.

RYAN: No! Stop! You picked up a triangular pyramid. It has a triangle base and three congruent faces. That's not what the voices said. Here. Use this one instead. It's a square pyramid. This is the key.

NARRATOR: Tran picked up the square pyramid. He reached out with it and touched the portal shaped like a cube. Suddenly, lightning flashed! With a loud roar, the portal opened up, and another new galaxy appeared in front of them. Everyone hurried into the spaceship. Just as they flew through the portal, the giant computer screen turned on.

DOOMSDAY ALIENS: Too bad for you and your friends, Princess! We flew through the second portal 30 minutes ago. Soon, the treasure will be ours on Planet AU79. We will be the new rulers of the universe. Ha, ha, ha, ha, ha!

NARRATOR: The spaceship landed again, and the friends hurried outside.

RYAN: Don't any of these planets have an ice cream shop? The first thing I'm going to do when I get my share of the treasure is buy a double pistachio!

VOICES: This key has similarities to the previous key,
but its base is a circle, not a square.
It's time to choose the perfect key
that will take you away from here.

TRAN: Wait! They're so cunning that they didn't tell us which portal to choose.

TRON: They only told us the key is shaped like a cone, so how are we supposed to make an accurate guess?

RYAN: What are we going to do, Princess? We don't want to be exterminated after coming this far.

PRINCESS SASHA: We must choose wisely. One portal is shaped like a cone. The other is shaped like a square pyramid. At the first portal, the shape of the key matched the shape of the portal. Our future existence depends on this choice, but I . . . think . . . we should do the opposite from before, so let's choose the portal that *doesn't* match the key.

NARRATOR: Princess Sasha picked up the key shaped like a cone. She touched it to the portal shaped like a square pyramid. They all held their breath. Suddenly, lightning flashed! With a loud roar, the portal opened up, and another new galaxy appeared in front of them. Everyone hurried into the spaceship. As they flew through the portal, the giant computer screen turned on.

DOOMSDAY ALIENS: Oh no! We chose the wrong key! We chose the wrong portal! Now we're doomed to float around forever locked in cubes of nothingness. A-a-a-a-h-h-h-h!

NARRATOR: Princess Sasha and her friends cheered! Now the gold, jewels, and treasure would be theirs! Just then they landed on the next planet, so they hurried outside and stood before the two portals.

VOICES: This is the ultimate and final portal. On the other side of the correct portal are zillions of riches. If you choose the wrong portal, however, you will be frozen in a sphere of ice for 1,000 years. Choose the key shaped like a cylinder and choose the matching portal. Then the treasure will be yours.

PRINCESS SASHA: This one is easy! They told us which key and which portal to choose. And they match! Here, X4B4, give me the box of keys.

X4B4: That's it. That is the last time I will miss out on all the excitement. I am going to choose the key myself and open this portal. It's about time I get to do something fun, too.

RYAN: But X4B4, that's not the right key! That's not a cylinder—you're holding a sphere! And you're touching the portal that looks like a sphere. That's the wrong one!

TRAN: Don't do it, X4B4!

TRON: Put it back in the box, X4B4!

NARRATOR: It was too late. A ghastly noise sounded. The portal opened wide and sucked everyone inside.

RYAN: Help! I'm free-ee-eezing . . .

NARRATOR: Suddenly, everyone was frozen in a sphere of ice.

Scene 2: 1,000 Years Later, in the Year 4456

NARRATOR: All at once, the ice melted and everyone was standing next to the spaceship.

PRINCESS SASHA: Wh-what happened?

TRAN: Don't you remember? X4B4 picked the wrong key and inserted it into the portal before we could stop him.

TRON: Yeah, I thought we were exterminated. Wiped out. Gone.

RYAN: That's right. Now I remember. Maybe we get a second chance, so this time we'll choose the right key, the one that's shaped like a cylinder. Here, X4B4, let me see the box of keys.

X4B4: Why certainly, dear friend. Your wish is my command! My, isn't it a bright and sunny day in this corner of the universe?

PRINCESS SASHA: The 1,000 years in ice must have frozen his circuit panels!

NARRATOR: Ryan took the cylinder and opened the portal. There, spread out before them, was an entire planet filled with gold, jewels, and other treasures. Everyone cheered.

PRINCESS SASHA: Thank you, kind friends, for helping me find my treasure. I'll give you each an equal share of one million dollars so you may go back to your Planet Earth and live like royalty.

NARRATOR: The three friends collected their share of the treasure and headed home. When they reached Planet Earth, they went straight to the ice cream shop.

RYAN: I'd like a double pistachio with butterscotch on top, please. It's my favorite!

ICE CREAM WORKER: Here you are. One ice cream cone. That will be one million dollars. Who's next?

RYAN: A million dollars? What do you mean? An ice cream cone only costs one dollar!

ICE CREAM WORKER: Where have you been for the last 1,000 years, kid? Were you frozen out in space or something? An ice cream cone costs one million dollars. Now give me your money, and let your two friends take a turn!

POSSIBLE EXTENSIONS

1. Create a group of Doomsday Aliens to display in class. Either collect empty boxes to make the project at school or ask students to build their galactic creatures at home. Use cereal boxes or shoeboxes as rectangular prisms. Square facial tissue boxes may be used as cubes. Oatmeal or potato chip boxes may be used as cylinders. Add cone-shaped party hats and paper towel tubes for extra dimension. Instruct students to cover their boxes with gift wrap, brown paper bags, and butcher paper before building their aliens and to paint them with poster paints when completed. Allow time for students to share their aliens with the class, identifying which shapes they used.

2. Play a solid figures guessing game called "What Am I?" Divide the class into teams of four or five students each. Give clues about one shape, such as, "I have six faces. I have eight vertexes. All my edges are congruent." Allow time for each team to discuss the answer and draw a picture of the solid figure. Each team that guesses correctly wins a point.

3. Introduce Marshmallow Math to students. Give each student 20 miniature marshmallows and 30 wooden toothpicks. Instruct them to build a cube, a triangular pyramid, and a square pyramid. When they are finished, allow them to construct a 3-dimensional shape of their choice.

4. Create a matching card game for students to play with during free time. Using index cards, make two or three matching cards for each solid shape. According to students' skill levels, one card can be a picture of a solid shape, one card can be the name of that solid shape, and one card can be the description of that solid shape with optional formulas. To play the game, spread the cards out face down. Students take turns turning over two or three cards at a time (depending on the number of matching ones in a set). When a match is found, students keep those cards. The player with the most cards at the end of the game wins.

5. Use a set of translucent plastic geometric solids with removable sides to allow students time to explore solid shapes. This set can be filled with wet or dry materials to compare volume, weight, and other attributes of solid shapes. Look for a set at your local teacher supply store or at www.educationallearninggames.com/3-D-geometry-game.asp.

CHAPTER 5

Fraction Olympics
(Fractions)

STAGING: Seat Announcers 1 and 2 on stools at the front left of the stage. The Crowd may be seated across the back of the stage. Dawn Divider and Felipe Factor may sit at the front right of the stage and exit the stage when their turns are over. The Bobsled Driver, Bobsled Brakeman, and Bobsled Pushers 1 and 2 should wait offstage until their turns. Nancy Numerator and Darin Denominator should also wait offstage until their turns.

CHARACTERS

Announcers 1 and 2	Bobsled Driver
Crowd	Bobsled Brakeman
Dawn Divider	Darin Denominator
Felipe Factor	Nancy Numerator
Bobsled Pushers 1 and 2	

```
                          Crowd
                          X X X


                                      Dawn          Felipe
                                      Divider       Factor
                                      X             X

      Announcers 1 and 2
           X    X
```

Fraction Olympics

ANNOUNCER 1: Thanks for joining us, folks! We're here high up on the slopes of Mount Fraction. The top half is covered with snow.

ANNOUNCER 2: Welcome to the Winter Olympics. Every event is full of action, and split second maneuvers determine who gets the gold medal. It's a whole lot of fun, fun, fun!

ANNOUNCER 1: This first event takes place here on the slopes. The crowd is going wild. Listen to them shriek and shout.

CROWD: Three cheers for the Winter Olympics! Bravo for Mount Fraction!

ANNOUNCER 2: Will their favorite champion, Dawn Divider, win the gold medal once more?

ANNOUNCER 1: Three-fourths of the crowd says she will!

ANNOUNCER 2: One-fourth of the crowd is cheering for the underdog, Felipe Factor. They say he's the greatest common factor the world has ever seen!

ANNOUNCER 1: We'll find out soon enough. They're getting ready to start.

CROWD: They're off! Look at them go! We're in awe of such speed.

ANNOUNCER 2: They're hurtling down the snowy slopes, racing to the finish line.

CROWD: Hip, hip hooray! Such fantastic moves!

ANNOUNCER 1: Dawn Divider crossed the finish line in 12/24 minutes flat.

ANNOUNCER 2: But wait! Felipe Factor crossed the finish line in 9/18 minutes.

ANNOUNCER 1: It's a tie! This year we have two champions for this event.

ANNOUNCER 2: And now we have BOTH winners here to tell us how they did it.

 From *Hello Hi-Lo: Readers Theatre Math* by Jeff Sanders and Nancy I. Sanders. Santa Barbara, CA: Libraries Unlimited. Copyright © 2010.

DAWN DIVIDER:	It was simple for me. I always divide both the numerator and the denominator by the same number. I keep dividing until that fraction is in simplest form.
ANNOUNCER 1:	Was it harder than last year?
DAWN DIVIDER:	I knew the course this year was going to be intense the whole way down the slope.
ANNOUNCER 2:	How did you know?
DAWN DIVIDER:	Mount Fractions is one of the steepest slopes in the world. It has fractions so big that I had to keep dividing every turn I took. Finally, though, I knew there were no other numbers to use. Only 1 would divide into both the top and the bottom of the fractions. At that point, I crossed the finish line.
FELIPE FACTOR:	I used a totally different strategy. I knew it would be tough coming against a returning champion, so first I made two lists. One list includes the factors of the numerator. The second list includes the factors of the denominator.
ANNOUNCER 1:	Is that all it took to fly down the slopes with such effective speed?
FELIPE FACTOR:	No. As I neared the finish line, I knew I had to do my best if I wanted to get the gold. I looked at my lists and determined the greatest common factor. Then I divided both the numerator and the denominator by that number. That's when I crossed the finish line.
ANNOUNCER 2:	And that's when you both got the same answer you'd been looking for! You both found that fraction in simplest form at the exact same time while speeding down the snowy slopes of Mount Fraction.
ANNOUNCER 1:	Your two methods were both a winner. You both crossed the finish line in exactly half a minute.
ANNOUNCER 2:	It's a tie! Congratulations.
ANNOUNCER 1:	Now we have another exciting race. Who will gain this victory?
ANNOUNCER 2:	Next up on the Winter Olympics is the Bobsled. The first four-man team is lined up and ready to go. They're off!

ANNOUNCER 1: They're two-thirds of the way down the straights.

CROWD: Go, go, go! We're amazed. What a fast start!

ANNOUNCER 2: Now they're facing some of the sharpest turns in Olympic history.

ANNOUNCER 1: This sled is moving so rapidly, it's hard to see. What a team!

ANNOUNCER 2: Can you believe it? They just flew past the finish line. It's a new world record! And we saw it today at Mount Fraction. Here they are to tell us how it happened.

BOBSLED BRAKEMAN: The straights were the same here as they are everywhere. But when we rounded the first turn, there were mixed numbers all over the place. I had to brake. But then we decided to multiply them to pick up our speed. We knew right away that all these mixed numbers needed to be rewritten as improper fractions first. That's the way to multiply mixed numbers with lightning speed.

BOBSLED PUSHERS 1 AND 2: As we headed to the finish line, everything was all mixed up. We had fractions, mixed numbers, and decimals. We pushed from the left. Then we pushed from the right. That's when we decided to use a number line to get straight down the snowy slope as fast as possible.

BOBSLED DRIVER: As the driver, I had to work fast. I wrote each fraction, mixed number, and decimal on a number line. Then I compared the results. That's how I knew what order everything was from least to greatest. That's when we crossed the finish line.

ANNOUNCER 1: Plus, you set a new world record. This was no accident.

ANNOUNCER 2: It took quick thinking, teamwork, and experience with fractions. Congratulations. You're the best in history!

ANNOUNCER 1: Next we have the third and final show of the season, figure skating. Cheer your hardest. This pair deserves your best.

40

ANNOUNCER 2: These champion skaters have been performing here at the top half of Mount Fraction for the better part of these last two weeks. They're here right now for their final performance in this exhibition gala.

ANNOUNCER 1: It's a skating-crazed crowd we have here today. Their favorite pair of figure skaters has to get the highest score. That's if they want to win the gold this year.

CROWD: We love you, Nancy Numerator and Darin Denominator!

ANNOUNCER 2: Can Nancy Numerator and Darin Denominator dance their way to figure skating victory? They've been skating together as a fraction for three years now. Do they have what it takes to write their score as a decimal? Hold your breath because the music has started to play!

CROWD: Go for the gold! Build up your momentum and dance your way to the winning score!

ANNOUNCER 1: The crowd is cheering as this fraction team spins and dances its way over the ice.

ANNOUNCER 2: Look at that amazing footwork as Darin Denominator lifts Nancy Numerator in the air. What an amazing jump! Not a stumble, not a miss. Everything is perfectly in beat to the lyrical music.

CROWD: What a fantastic routine. What complex moves. Hip, hip hooray!

ANNOUNCER 1: The music has stopped. So has our favorite fraction team of figure skaters. The judges are busy adding up the score. Will they be our new champions?

ANNOUNCER 2: They won! Their total score was 184.63. They're tops! And here they both are to share how they won the gold.

NANCY NUMERATOR: We've been skating as a fraction for a long time. We knew what to do today on the ice.

DARIN DENOMINATOR: We know that any fraction can be written as a decimal. That's because fractions and decimals are related.

ANNOUNCER 1: Was it during that first spin that you made your first move toward victory?

41

**DARIN
DENOMINATOR:** Yes. I knew I had to change the first fraction into a decimal. As I spun Nancy around on the ice, I multiplied the fraction so it had the denominator of 100. Then it was a simple matter to write it as a decimal.

ANNOUNCER 2: It was amazing!

NANCY NUMERATOR: The next fraction was very hard, so Darin and I planned a jump.

**DARIN
DENOMINATOR:** That's right! Fractions are great to work with. You can also divide the numerator by the denominator to get a decimal. I lifted Nancy high in the air.

NANCY NUMERATOR: That's when we made our jump to victory and got the score!

ANNOUNCER 1: Our champions know how to handle fractions with skill and ease.

ANNOUNCER 2: Congratulations Darin and Nancy. And congratulations to all our winners here today on Mount Fraction at the Winter Olympics. Thank you for joining us for a whole day of fun, fun, fun!

POSSIBLE EXTENSIONS

1. Make a bulletin board with a ski slope on it. Mount paper flags all along the ski slope, large enough to write on. Write a different fraction to reduce on each paper flag according to your students' abilities. Instruct students to write each fraction in simplest form.

   Change the fractions on the flags for different exercises. For instance, one day you could write a mixed number on each flag and have students write each as an improper fraction.

2. Host your own Fraction Olympics. Divide students into small groups or teams of five members each. Each team can represent a different event at the Olympics. Assign each team a different type of fraction problem such as addition, multiplication, lowest terms, or positive and negative. Have each team write down five different problems, each on a separate index card. (They may choose examples from the book or create their own.) Tell members of the team to work together to solve their problems on scrap paper, then write the correct answers on the back of the corresponding index cards.

   When the class is ready, host the Fraction Olympics. Invite the first team to write their problems on the board as the other teams solve them. Each team that answers correctly scores a point. When the first team is finished, invite a second team to write their problems on the board. Continue until every team has a turn to write their problems on the board. The team with the most points wins. As an extra bonus, award every team member of all the teams a foil-covered gold chocolate coin. (When serving food, always be sensitive to food allergies your students might have.)

3. Provide paper and craft supplies to let students create models or posters that compare various fractions. Examples include but are not limited to graphs, charts, and a number line. Display finished fraction projects.

4. Assign a writing project to explore fractions in real life. As a class, brainstorm a list of places and situations in which we find fractions in our world. Invite volunteers to share examples such as eating pizza, serving an apple pie, baking with measuring cups, or measuring. Write these ideas in a list on the board. When finished, instruct students to each choose one example and write a real-life story that involves fractions.

CHAPTER 6

The World Book of Amazing Records (Decimals)

STAGING: Seat the Publisher in the front center of the stage. Peng the Panda may be seated just behind him on the left of the stage. The Panda Bears may be seated in a group just behind the publisher on the right of the stage. The rest of the characters should wait offstage until their turns to speak. When it is time for each new scene, the new characters may enter the stage and take their places as the previous ones exit.

CHARACTERS

Publisher

Panda Bears

Peng the Panda

Kangaroos

Kandi the Kangaroo

Mountain Goats

Max the Mountain Goat

Peng the Panda
X

Pandas
X X X X

Publisher
X

The World Book of Amazing Records

Scene 1: China

PUBLISHER: I'm here in China searching for the biggest records to add to the *World Book of Amazing Records*. This year we've ratcheted up the competition a decimal or two. We're looking for world-class acts.

PANDA BEARS: Who do you have your eye on here in China? Have you been to the Great Wall of China yet? We heard in the news that there's a bird who flies the entire length of the wall.

PUBLISHER: I've heard of that bird, but even though he can accomplish that amazing feat in just 248.25 hours, that's not who I'm here to see.

PANDA BEARS: Are you here to see the tiger who can do 2.5 flips in one leap?

PUBLISHER: The Siberian Tiger?

PANDA BEARS: That's the one. He's known all over the world for his amazing leap.

PUBLISHER: He made it in the *World Book of Amazing Records* last year. No, I'm not looking for him. This year I'm looking for a panda who can balance 300.99 teacups on his forehead for 3.5 days straight.

PENG THE PANDA: I'm here! I was hoping you were here looking for me. How did you hear of me? Did you read my biography? Who told you what I could do?

PUBLISHER: News gets around pretty fast in this market. I came straight to China as soon as I heard of your extraordinary talent. Could you show me a demonstration?

PENG THE PANDA: Of course! My panda pals will help me get set up. It's not easy stacking hundreds of cups on my forehead.

PUBLISHER: I have just one question to ask before you begin. Why are you known for balancing 300.99 teacups on your forehead? Why not 301?

PENG THE PANDA: One of the teacups broke and a small chip fell out. I had a hunch it wouldn't be right to count it as a whole cup.

PUBLISHER: You're right! With decimals, accuracy is tops. Get the point?

PANDA BEARS: Hey! We have a question. We heard that another panda bear might take the new world record. Is that true?

PUBLISHER: You mean Patei the Panda? He didn't even come close! He can only balance 30.099 teacups on his forehead.

PANDA BEARS: Isn't that the exact same number, though?

PUBLISHER: It's not even close. I look for new world records by comparing the place value. Look where the decimal point is. It makes all the difference when you look at the digits of a decimal number. 300.99 and 30.099 are two totally different animals.

Scene 2: Australia

PUBLISHER: Today I'm here in Australia. Peng the Panda made it into my *World Book of Amazing Records*. Now I'm looking for a kangaroo.

KANGAROOS: Good day, mate! It's nice to see you in the world down under. What brings you here to this dusty side of the outback down here where the koala bears hang out?

PUBLISHER: I've heard of a kangaroo who can jump so high it looks like she's hopping clear up to the sky. We're not talking 3.915 feet high like last year's world record. We're singing to the tune of 39.15 feet up in the air for every jump she takes.

KANGAROOS: You must be looking for Kandi the Kangaroo. She's a legend in these parts. We'll give her a call and let her know you're here. She always keeps her cell phone in her pocket now that she's a celebrity. Everyone wants to talk with her.

PUBLISHER:	Let her know I want to see her right away. It could be worth $1958.00 if she's as good as she sounds. And I'm not talking about $19.58 like we paid our winner last year. This year we increased the award money up a decimal or two.
KANDI THE KANGAROO:	Hi, mates! Thanks for calling me and letting me know you wanted to see me. What do you want?
PUBLISHER:	I've heard you can jump up 39.15 feet in the air and catch a boomerang with your bare paws.
KANDI THE KANGAROO:	That's right, mate. I've been practicing, too. Now I can jump even higher and beat my own world record.
PUBLISHER:	Let's view a demonstration, because I'm ready to start immediately. Will one of you kangaroos throw a boomerang?
KANGAROOS:	We'll toss that bird up in the air and help out with this exciting event in any way that we can. Here it goes, mate.
KANDI THE KANGAROO:	Okay! I'm jumping. I'm jumping. I'm jumping! It always takes me a few jumps to get the really big bounce that I need. Here I go!
KANGAROOS:	Look at that jump! And what a fantastic catch!
PUBLISHER:	I wouldn't have believed it if I didn't see it with my very own eyes. Congratulations, Kandi! Your jump of 40.02 feet qualifies for my *World Book of Amazing Records*! You win the prize of $1,958.00.
KANDI THE KANGAROO:	Thank you so much. I'm so excited to be in your book of world records.

Scene 3: Switzerland

PUBLISHER:	Now I'm here in Switzerland to find the last winner for my new *World Book of Amazing Records*.

48

MOUNTAIN GOATS: May we help you? Not many people climb all the way up here because these Swiss mountains are at the top of the world.

PUBLISHER: I'm looking for a goat who can yodel. I heard he hangs out here at the Matterhorn.

MOUNTAIN GOATS: You must mean Max. He's famous around here and is known as a celebrity. No matter how much ice, wind, or snow there is, he's in fine voice. Look! Here he comes now. Hey, Max! There's somebody here to see you.

MAX THE MOUNTAIN GOAT: Sorry, but I can't talk now. I'm saving my voice for my next big yodel.

PUBLISHER: But that's why I came here to find you! I want to hear you yodel!

MAX THE MOUNTAIN GOAT: You're in luck, then, because I'm scheduled to start yodeling in just 2.25 minutes.

PUBLISHER: How long can you hold a yodel?

MAX THE MOUNTAIN GOAT: I'm going for a new world record today of 22.5 minutes without taking a single breath.

PUBLISHER: Do you really think you can do it? That kind of accomplishment takes a pair of lungs with an enormous air capacity.

MAX THE MOUNTAIN GOAT: This mountain air helps build strong lungs. That's why I yodel at the top of the Matterhorn. It keeps me in top shape. I'm sorry that I can't talk any longer. I have to climb the Matterhorn and get ready to yodel. Good-bye.

PUBLISHER: But how will I know how long he yodels? Should I climb the Matterhorn, too?

MOUNTAIN GOATS: Of course not! Max is so loud you'll be able to hear him right where you are. In fact, if you stand too close to him, it's just too loud. He reaches the high decimals and before you know it, your ears hurt. It's that loud.

PUBLISHER: Look! I can see him climbing the Matterhorn now! See? He's the goat with the hat.

MOUNTAIN GOATS: We see him. But how will you measure how long he yodels? What if he yodels for 22.50 minutes? Or what if he yodels for 22.500 minutes? That would really be something.

PUBLISHER: Not really. You can add as many zeroes as you want to the right of the decimal at the end of the number and it won't change a thing. 22.5 minutes is the same as 22.50 minutes is the same as 22.500 minutes.

MOUNTAIN GOATS: How can you be so sure about all these decimals?

PUBLISHER: I compare decimals all the time. That's how I know who the winners are for my *World Book of Amazing Records.* For instance, I know which digits are in the hundreds place and which ones are in the hundredths place.

MOUNTAIN GOATS: It sounds like there's a big difference between the two, but it's just part of your job, right?

PUBLISHER: That's right. I use place value to order the decimal numbers from the least to the greatest. That's how I know who the winners are each year. That's how I know Max is the winner this year. No other goat can yodel like Max—not even the Three Billy Goats Gruff.

MOUNTAIN GOATS: Didn't they win the Swiss Idol this year?

PUBLISHER: Yes. They're a sensational act. They may have class, but they don't have the decimals I'm looking for. I only go for the biggest decimals of all.

POSSIBLE EXTENSIONS

1.   Create an interactive bulletin board to practice place-value skills with decimals. To prepare, distribute blank index cards to your class and instruct students to each use every numeral from 0 to 9 and write a decimal number of their choice, for example, 83.01624579, 19823.70465, or 56743829.01.

   Mount these cards along the bottom of the bulletin board. Across the top of the board, write in large letters: These decimals have a _____ in the _____ place. Each day, post a new card in each blank space. For instance, one day it could read: *These decimals have a 6 in the hundreds place.* The next day you can change it to read: *These decimals have a 0 in the tenths place.* Have students examine the decimals posted across the bottom of the board each day and choose the corresponding ones to move and mount up above in the center of the board.

2.   Play a game of Decimal Scramble. First, prepare two empty one-dozen egg cartons with lids by opening the lid of each egg carton and numbering the back row of cups from 1 to 6. Number the front row of cups from 6 to 1. (Write each number on the bottom of each cup.) Place one marble or one dried bean inside each egg carton and close it.

   To play Decimal Scramble, two players each shake the marbles inside their egg cartons and then open them up. The marbles replace the number as a decimal point in the cups where they are sitting. Players should then only read the decimal numbers in the row where the marbles have landed. For instance, if the marble is in the back row and in the cup numbered 4, that player's number is 123.56. If the marble is in the front row and in the cup numbered 6, that player's number is .54321. Instruct students to compare their decimals. The one with the decimal of greatest value scores one point. If there is a tie, both students score one point. Repeat nine more times. After ten turns, the player with the most points wins the game. You may vary this game by awarding points for the decimal of lowest value.

3.   Create a center for students to visit in their spare time where they can practice comparing decimals. Prepare by writing three decimals with matching digits that each have a decimal point in a different position, for example, 40.397, 4.0397, and 403.97. Make 10 sets of three cards each. Create an answer key with each set in order from greatest to least or from least to greatest. Invite students to visit the center, sort the cards into similar sets, and put them in order as directed. Have them check their work against the answer key.

4.   Play a fast-paced game to change fractions to decimals or decimals to fractions. Divide the class into two teams. Have the first player on each team come to the board and write a decimal or fraction on the board, such as .502. The first student to write it correctly as a fraction wins a point for his or her team. If there is a tie, both teams score a point. Have the second player on each team come to the board. Repeat the activity until every student has a turn. The team with the most points at the end wins the game.

5.   Practice using money to gain practical experience working with decimals. Create an imaginary store on a bulletin board by posting pictures of various items from magazines and assigning each one a price tag according to the skill level you are teaching your students. Inform students that they each have a certain amount of money to spend, such as $100 or $250. Give them guidelines, such as that they must purchase multiples of some items (to practice multiplication skills) and must spend as much of their money as possible without overspending. Instruct them to keep an account of which items they purchase at what price and record the total sum. When finished, allow time for students to discuss results.

6.   To assess students' comprehension, ask them to either write in their journal or explain in their own words key concepts about decimals. Use prompts like these:

– Demonstrate . . .

– Tell in your own words . . .

– Give an example of . . .

– Why is this a different value than . . .

– Describe . . .

– Show how . . .

– What does it mean when . . .

CHAPTER 7

Talk Like a Gentleman Day (Equations)

STAGING: Captain Jack and the First Mate should be standing together, center stage. Cabin Boys 1 and 2 may stand along the left side of the stage. The crew may stand across the back of the stage.

CHARACTERS

Captain Jack	Crew
First Mate	Cabin Boys 1 and 2

```
                         Crew
                  X      X       X



      Cabin Boys 1, 2
        X   X
                        Captain Jack      First Mate
                             X                 X
```

Talk Like a Gentleman Day

Setting: On a Pirate's Ship Sailing the Seven Seas

CAPTAIN JACK: Today is a special holiday, mateys. Once a year it's "Talk Like a Gentleman Day." So as your captain, I'm commanding ye to speak proper today.

FIRST MATE: But Captain, the ship's in desperate trouble. It got battered in that terrible storm that hit us yesterday. Our sails are in shreds. Even though it's a holiday, methinks I need all hands on deck to make new sails for the ship. Otherwise, we might be sinking to Davy Jones's locker if another storm blows in with the evening tide.

CAPTAIN JACK: Shiver me timbers! All right, then. Listen up, lads. There will be no rest on this holiday for the likes of you. All hands on deck to help the First Mate make new sails. Just remember, though! Be sure ye speak like a gentleman while ye work. I don't want to hear any scurvy dog talking like a pirate today. If I do, I'll send ye to sit in the lifeboat. Then tomorrow night there's a full moon. That's when that lifeboat's sinking down to Davy Jones's locker!

FIRST MATE: Where are ye going now, Captain Jack?

CAPTAIN JACK: I'm going below deck. But when I come back, I'll be checking all ye rascals. If ye are not talking like a gentleman, tomorrow night it's Davy Jones's locker for ye!

CREW: Aye, aye, Captain! See ye later.

[Exit Captain Jack.]

FIRST MATE: Gather round, buccaneers! First we'll hoist the skull and crossbones. Cabin boys, fly those colors proper now while we work.

CABIN BOY 1: Shiver me timbers! The flag's shredded to bits, too. We'll be needing a new skull and crossbones to fly.

FIRST MATE: Then make one. Put your heart into it, lads, be sure 'tis the same size as the first. If ye remember, the first skull and crossbones was in the shape of a rectangle, and the short sides were both equal. Its other two longer sides were equal, too. They each were twice as long as the shorter sides. If the perimeter of the flag is 12 feet, what is the measurement of the short side?

CABIN BOY 2: Avast, now. We don't know how this is done. How can we figure this out?

FIRST MATE: Make an equation, ye scalawags. Can't ye see? Here, first draw a picture of the skull and crossbones. It will help ye. Draw a rectangle.

CABIN BOY 1: Confound it, ye yellow-belly of a pirate dog! What's the next step to take?

FIRST MATE: Now choose a letter. This letter is called the variable. Try "s" for skull and crossbones. "S" is a good letter. This variable will help ye remember you are figuring the side of the skull and crossbones.

CABIN BOY 2: Methinks we still do not know what to do.

FIRST MATE: You're doing good, lads. Now label your drawing with the variable. Write down all the information ye know about that rectangle. That will help ye write the equation. But wait, here comes the captain!

[Enter Captain Jack.]

CABIN BOY 1: X marks the spot! It worked! Drawing a picture and using a letter really helped. Thank ye, ye salty dog.

CAPTAIN JACK: Arrr! What's this I hear? Cabin boys, you're not talking proper like. I don't hear ye talking like a gentleman should. Defend yourselves, lads.

CABIN BOY 2: Yo ho ho! Methinks we got the equation right. We're the happiest lads to ever sail the high seas.

CAPTAIN JACK: Don't ye remember? This is a holiday. It's "Talk Like a Gentleman Day." You are still talking like a pirate. It's off to the lifeboat with ye. Tomorrow night, ye both will be sinking to Davy Jones's locker!

FIRST MATE: But Captain, these lads here just figured out how to make us yellow-bellied rascals a new skull and crossbones.

CAPTAIN JACK: But they weren't talking proper like. Watch yourself, or I'll have ye walking the plank. Now get these scurvy dogs back to work making new sails. I'm going to check on the cook. When I come back, I'll be checking all ye rascals. If ye are not talking like a gentleman, it's Davy Jones's locker for ye!

CREW: Aye, aye, captain! See ye later.

[Exit Captain Jack.]

FIRST MATE: Gather round, buccaneers! It's time to make new sails. Some sails are squares, some sails are triangles, and some sails are rectangles. Now get to work and make these sails.

CREW: But how? We don't have all the measurements. This is the dirtiest and sneakiest trick of all. How can we figure this out? A number is missing on one side for each sail.

FIRST MATE: Now drop your anchor and listen up. Don't you remember how I told the other lads that ye need to write an equation to figure out the missing numbers?

CREW: We'd give our best eye patch and a peg leg to know how to write an equation. We don't know how.

FIRST MATE: Plunder me treasure chest! Weren't ye listening at all? First decide which number is missing on the first sail. Is it the length, is it the width, or is it one of the sides of the triangle?

CREW: Ahoy, matey. We see which number is missing. It's the length.

FIRST MATE: Now pick a letter, or a variable, to use for the missing number.

CREW: All right. We pick "l" for length. But we still feel like we're shipwrecked.

FIRST MATE: That's because now ye have to draw a picture to help figure it out. Draw a picture of the sail ye are working on. Label each side of the sail with the numbers ye know and the variable ye are looking for. But avast now. Here's the captain coming back again.

[Enter Captain Jack.]

CREW: Yo ho ho! It worked! Drawing a picture helped us figure it out. Now we can write the equation. Thank ye, ye salty dog.

CAPTAIN JACK: Arrr! What's this I hear? Buccaneers, ye are not talking proper like. I don't hear ye talking like a gentleman should. Defend yourselves.

CREW: Methinks we got the equation right. Now we can make the sails. We're as happy as if we found some gold dubloons.

CAPTAIN JACK: Don't ye remember? This is a holiday. It's "Talk Like a Gentleman Day." You are still talking like a pirate. It's off to the lifeboat for the lot of ye. And ye, too, First Mate. Tomorrow night, it's Davy Jones's locker for ye!

FIRST MATE: But Captain! Ye are not talking like a gentleman, either. Ye are still talking like a lily-livered pirate.

CAPTAIN JACK: Shiver me timbers, you're right!

FIRST MATE: What are we to do? The whole pirate crew will be sinking to Davy Jones's locker when the full moon rises tomorrow, including the captain.

CAPTAIN JACK: Not if I have my way. From now on I'm making a new holiday. Tomorrow will be "Talk Like a Pirate Day." Every rascal who talks like a pirate tomorrow gets to join my crew. Captain too, I says, says I. No more Davy Jones's locker for me and my pirate crew.

CREW: Yo ho ho! Three cheers for "Talk Like a Pirate Day"!

POSSIBLE EXTENSIONS

1. Create an Equation Match Game. Use 15 index cards to create five sets of matches. Each set should include one equation, one picture of that equation, and one word problem for that equation.

    Players play in pairs. Each player turns over three cards to take a turn. If all three cards represent the same equation, it's a match. The player collects those three cards and takes another turn. The player with the most cards at the end wins the game.

2. On a bulletin board, mount a large picture of a pirate's ship. Be sure to have at least five or six sails on the ship. Use a variety of geometric shapes for the sails, such as triangles, squares, and rectangles. Write a different equation on each sail, according to the ability of your students. For extra credit, invite students to solve each equation. Change the equations daily.

3. September 19 is International Talk Like a Pirate Day. Celebrate this fun holiday with your students. Ideas include the following:

    – Dress like a pirate.

    – Make every math problem pirate related.

    – Decorate your room with a pirate's theme.

    – Award gold foil chocolate "coins" or treats from a treasure chest.

    – And of course, invite everyone to talk like a pirate!

4. Play a math game similar to the game Probe. First use index cards to make four sets of matching cards. Each set should include 14 cards, labeled with the numbers 1 through 9, +, -, ÷ , x, and =. Write one character on each card. Add one or more cards with variables such as n, a, or b, according to the ability of your students. Add five blank cards to each set. Each set will have at least 20 cards in it, and more if you add more than one variable.

    Prepare four game boards. To make a game board, cut a 12-by-18-inch piece of construction paper in half lengthwise. Tape these together end to end. Divide them into 8 to 10 equal segments from left to right so that one index card can be placed in each segment. Assign each segment a different point value, such as 1 point, 3 points, 5 points, 10 points, and 15 points. Assign these values randomly; some spaces may be worth the same number of points. When finished with the first game board, make three more that match.

    To set up the game, two to four players sit side by side at a long table or on the floor. Each player should sit with his or her game board in front. Demonstrate how each player should choose some of his or her cards and secretly place them facedown on the game board to form an equation. Each equation must include one or more variables, according to the skill level you are teaching. Examples of equations follow:

    $$2n + 9 = 87$$

    $$81 - 32 = 4b$$

    $$5 \text{ x } 6 = 8b$$

    Blanks may be placed in front of or after the equation to trick the other players, but they must not be placed in the middle of the equation. The equation may start at the end of the game board or in the middle, according to the decision of each player. Not every space on the game board has to have an index card in it.

    To play the game, students take turns asking if one of the other players has a certain card. For instance, one player might ask the player to his right, "Do you have a 9?" If the player has a "9" on her board, she must turn it face-up in its spot. If the first player guessed correctly, he gets another turn. He might then ask the player at the end, "Do you have a blank?" If that player has a "blank" on his board, he must turn it face-up in its spot. If the player on the end has more than one blank, he only has to turn over one of them at that turn.

Players earn points for each card they guess. The number of points they earn is determined by the point value of the space where the card is positioned on the game board. If a player asks for a blank and the second player has no blanks, the first player loses 10 points from her total score.

If a player guesses correctly, he gets another turn. If not, the turn goes to the player to his left. Play continues from player to player until every card is turned over on every player's board. At no time does any player drop out of the game, even if her own equation is already revealed.

For an extra bonus of 10 points for each equation, players may solve the other players' equations on a separate piece of paper. There will be mixed numbers, fractions, or decimals as answers to the equations. At the end of the game, the player with the most points wins.

CHAPTER 8

The Greatest Tug of War (Inequalities)

STAGING: Seat the four storytellers along the front of the stage. As an option, you can group several students standing together to read each storyteller's part in unison, spreading these groups across the front of the stage.

CHARACTERS

Storytellers 1, 2, 3, and 4

Storyteller 1	Storyteller 2	Storyteller 3	Storyteller 4
X	X	X	X

The Greatest Tug of War

STORYTELLER 1: Once upon a time, a long time ago, in a world far away, there was a great war that took place.

STORYTELLER 2: At that time in that world, there were no mountains, no valleys, no oceans, no lakes.

STORYTELLER 3: That world was shaped like a round, smooth sphere.

STORYTELLER 4: At that time, the only creatures that lived in that world were mice. Mice totally populated the world—they lived everywhere!

STORYTELLER 1: And so it happened that one day a mouse named Dilbert found a piece of string cheese. He had never seen such a beautiful piece of cheese before anywhere in that world.

STORYTELLER 2: At that time and in that world, mice could walk like people. They walked on their feet and used their paws as hands.

STORYTELLER 3: Dilbert picked up one end of the string cheese in his paws and started to carry it off. At that very moment, however, another mouse saw the piece of string cheese. His name was Rufus. He wanted it, too, so Rufus grabbed the other end of the string cheese with his paws.

STORYTELLER 4: And that is how on that very same day, the greatest tug of war in the entire history of that world began. "I declare myself King of String Cheese!" cried Dilbert, pulling as hard as he could.

STORYTELLER 1: But as he pulled, Rufus shouted back to him, "No, I'm declaring myself King! I get this cheese!" And Rufus pulled harder still.

STORYTELLER 2: Each of the two mice pulled as hard as he could. But the number of both mice was equal on both sides of the string cheese.

STORYTELLER 3: So nothing happened. Word soon got around to all the mice about what was happening. Before long, three mice wearing helmets and carrying shields ran up to Dilbert.

STORYTELLER 4: "We will join the tug of war!" they squeaked as they joined King Dilbert's side and pulled. Now the number of mice on King Dilbert's side was greater than the number on the other side. They pulled the string cheese their way.

STORYTELLER 1: Just then two fair maiden mice scampered up to the other side. "Oh, King Rufus!" they cried. "We want you to be king of the world forever."

STORYTELLER 2: So they joined King Rufus's side and pulled on the string cheese with their paws. The fair maiden mice pulled and pulled with all their strength.

STORYTELLER 3: But there were only three mice on King Rufus's side, and there were four mice on King Dilbert's side. So the number of mice on King Rufus's side was less than the number on the other side. King Rufus called for more help! This time five strong mice joined his team. They pulled and they pulled on the string cheese with all their might!

STORYTELLER 4: Now there were eight mice on King Rufus's side. The number on King Rufus's side was now greater than the number on King Dilbert's side. But not for long! Suddenly a group of mice knights on elegant horses galloped up.

STORYTELLER 1: By now that world had horses in it. This group of mice knights jumped off their horses and joined King Dilbert's side. The number on King Dilbert's side was now greater than the number on King Rufus's side.

STORYTELLER 2: It looked like King Dilbert would win this tug of war. But then a new group of mice rode up.

STORYTELLER 3: This group of mice rode up on elephants. By now, that world had elephants in it, too. These mice joined King Rufus's side. Now the number on King Rufus's side was greater than the number on King Dilbert's side.

STORYTELLER 4: On and on, the tug of war raged. At times, the number on King Dilbert's side was greater than the number on King Rufus's side, and everyone thought that King Dilbert would win. But then more mice would join King Rufus and the number on King Dilbert's side would be less than the number on King Rufus's side.

STORYTELLER 1: Back and forth they went. Summer turned to fall. The rainy season came upon them, and the mice's feet slipped and slid through the mud.

STORYTELLER 2: Back and forth they went. They pulled and they tugged. They tugged and they pulled.

STORYTELLER 3: First one side's number was greater than the other side's. Then it would be less than the other side's. From all around that world, mice came to join the tug of war. Fall turned to winter and winter turned to spring.

STORYTELLER 4: By now there were cats in that world. The cats were amazed at this great tug of war. They watched and decided to write a mathematical equation about what was happening. They wanted to record it on paper for future generations to know about it.

STORYTELLER 1: The problem was that they could not write an equation.

STORYTELLER 2: The two sides were not equal!

STORYTELLER 3: The number of mice on one side was always greater than or less than the number on the other side.

STORYTELLER 4: Finally the cats decided what to do. They would write something they called an inequality! They would write a number sentence that showed how the two sides did not have the same value.

STORYTELLER 1: To do this, they had to think of a brand new way to show that one side was less than the other side. They needed a way to show that one side was greater than the other side.

STORYTELLER 2: At first they did not know how to do this. But one day a group of mice rode up to join the tug of war.

STORYTELLER 3: These mice were all riding on the strangest animal in that world the cats had ever seen. This animal was green and looked like a giant lizard.

STORYTELLER 4: At that time, this animal had the most dangerous mouth of all the creatures in all the world, for its mouth was filled with big, sharp teeth. The cats gave it the name "Alligator."

STORYTELLER 1: These new mice jumped off the alligator and joined King Dilbert's side. Now the number on King Dilbert's side was greater than the number on King Rufus's side. Just then the alligator opened its terrible mouth wide! The wide opening was toward King Dilbert's side. The wide opening was toward the number that was the greater.

STORYTELLER 2: Everyone stopped and stared at the great, big, wide open mouth. It looked like it wanted to eat all the mice on King Dilbert's side.

STORYTELLER 3: It was an amazing moment in the history of the world. The cats decided to write this down on a piece of paper.

STORYTELLER 4: It was the most important inequality of all time. And so it was that the cats had an inspiration. They decided to draw a symbol for the inequality that looked like an alligator's mouth. Just as the alligator's mouth was open wide toward the side with the greater number of mice, the symbol they used would open wide toward the side with the number that was greater than the other side.

STORYTELLER 1: As soon as the cats wrote this down, however, something else happened.

STORYTELLER 2: More mice rode up. They had come to join King Rufus's side.

STORYTELLER 3: These mice, however, were on a crocodile! These mice jumped off their crocodile and joined King Rufus's side. And for the very first time since the first two mice each pulled on the piece of string cheese, both sides were now equal!

STORYTELLER 4: Both sides now pulled so hard with equal strength that a great, deep crack cut apart in the ground. There was a huge noise such as the world had never heard, of grumblings and groanings and moanings from deep within the ground.

STORYTELLER 1: The string cheese stretched and stretched and stretched. The deep crack grew larger and larger. The two teams of mice were separated far away from each other. The string cheese was now so thin, it snapped!

STORYTELLER 2: Water rushed in to fill up the deep crack. Higher and higher the water came. Bigger and bigger the crack grew.

STORYTELLER 3: Now the two teams of mice were very far away from each other. They couldn't even see each other any more. The water in the crack sloshed back and forth and is still splashing in waves against the shores today.

STORYTELLER 4: And that is the story of how a great ocean came into being upon that world. Also, it is the story of how cats invented an inequality to show when two expressions do not have the same value. And that is also the story of why there are horses and alligators in some parts of that world and there are elephants and crocodiles in others, but there are mice and cats everywhere, just like in our world today.

The End

POSSIBLE EXTENSIONS

1. Create a center where students can practice simplifying expressions in an inequality. According to the skill level of your students, write an expression on an index card that does not contain a variable, such as 10 – (2 x 3). Write a variety of different expressions, each on a different index card, making sure that none of the answers is equal. Place all these index cards in a basket at the center along with paper and pencils.

    Use a 12-by-18-inch piece of construction paper to create a mat. Place the paper lengthwise like a hotdog in front of you on the table. Working from left to right, draw one rectangle, a symbol that means "is greater than," and then a second rectangle. (Each rectangle should be the same size as the index cards you are using so that when two index cards are placed in the two rectangles on the mat, they form a number sentence.) Make several mats for use at the center.

    When students visit the center, instruct them to choose a mat and two index cards from the basket. Have them simplify both expressions on scrap paper and then place the index cards on the mat on the corresponding side of the inequality symbol to form a correct number sentence. If two students visit the center together, they may check each other's work.

2. Play Math Tug of War with your students. Prepare by writing the numbers 1 to 10 on separate slips of paper and placing these all in a hat. Divide your class into two teams: King Dilbert's Team and King Rufus's Team. Invite one member from each team to come to the board. Position them to stand side by side.

    Start the story. Say: "Once upon a time, a long time ago, in a world far away, there was a great tug of war." Draw a number out of the hat. If it is a 3, say: "On King Dilbert's side there were 3 mice." Instruct the team member from that team to write the number 3 on the board. Draw a second number out of the hat. If it is a 5, say: "On King Rufus's side, there were 5 mice." Instruct the team member from that team to write the number 5 on the board. Ask both students to determine which inequality symbol (< or >) to write between the two numbers to show that 3 is less than 5. Have them write it on the board between the two numbers to form an inequality.

    Let the students return to their respective teams; return the numbers to the hat. Invite the next two team members up to the board to the same spot. Ask one of the students to make up the next part of the story about her own team. For instance, she might say: "Soon Olympic runner mice came scampering up to join our team." Then draw a number out of the hat to represent the number of mice that have joined her team. Have that student add that number to the current number on the board and write the new number in its place. Now ask the student from the other team to make up the next part of the story about his own team. For instance, he might say: "Then more mice rode up on dragons." Draw another number out of the hat to represent the number of mice that have joined his team. Have that student add that number to the current number on the board and write the new number in its place. Ask the students to determine together which symbol (< or >) to write between the two numbers to show the new inequality. Have them erase the first symbol and write the new one on the board.

    Continue to play this game with the rest of the students from each team. The game ends as a tie if both sides of the number sentence become equal. If not, the first team to get 25, 50, or 100 (depending on the amount of time you want to play the game) wins the Math Tug of War.

3. Prepare a bulletin board to practice and compare different number facts or expressions. Use a board big enough to mount two number facts or expressions as an inequality, such as 3 + 8 > 2 + 7. According to the skill you are teaching, prepare index cards with different number facts or expressions, one per card. Place these cards in a pocket on the bulletin board or in a nearby basket. Make separate cards for each inequality symbol (< or >) and pin these up on the side of the board.

Invite a student to choose two number facts or expressions from the index cards. Have her pin these to the board along with an inequality symbol (< or >) between them to form a true number sentence. Allow time for volunteers to change the number sentence at various times throughout your lesson. For older students, use a variety of symbols such as *greater than* or *equal to*, etc.

4. Play a game of Four Corners while learning how to graph inequalities. For the game, students stand in whichever corner of the room they choose. Using an overhead projector or Smart Board, display a graph on the board. Write down an inequality and simplify it or solve it. Then draw a graph of the inequality on the board.

    Assign each corner of the room to represent a different quadrant of the graph. All students standing in the corners that represent the numbers that are less than the others must sit down and are out of the game. These students may now follow along and graph the inequalities at their desks.

    Have students who are still in the game move to different corners of the room. Solve a second inequality and graph it on the board. Again, all students standing in the corners that represent the numbers that are less than the others must sit down and are out of the game. Continue playing until the last student (or two) is left and wins the game.

CHAPTER 9

A Colossal Surprise (Rounding)

STAGING: Seat the two government workers at the front center of the stage. The crowd may be seated across the back of the stage. The postal worker, shipping department worker, finance department worker, and builder may be sitting with the crowd at the back of the stage. When it is their turn to speak, they may each walk up to the front center of the stage and talk with the government workers. When finished, they should return to their seats among the crowd.

CHARACTERS

Government Workers 1 and 2

Postal Worker

Shipping Department Worker

Finance Department Worker

Builder

Crowd

```
                              Crowd
        X     X     X     X     X     X     X     X

     Postal        Shipping              Finance
     Worker        Department            Department         Builder
     X             Worker                Worker             X
                   X                     X



                 Government             Government
                 Worker 1               Worker 2
                 X                      X
```

A Colossal Surprise

POSTAL WORKER: I have a letter that just arrived from France, and it's marked urgent.

GOVERNMENT WORKER 1: Thanks for the special delivery. I appreciate your rush to get this here.

POSTAL WORKER: No problem. Have a good day, and I hope to see you again soon.

[Postal Worker exits.]

GOVERNMENT WORKER 1: If this is important, I should probably open this letter right away.

GOVERNMENT WORKER 2: What does it say? And why would France be writing to us in America?

GOVERNMENT WORKER 1: You'll never believe it! The letter says there's going to be a fantastic celebration. France has decided to give America a present. It's a great big giant colossal Statue of Liberty!

GOVERNMENT WORKER 2: What a surprise! How big is the statue? What else does the letter say?

GOVERNMENT WORKER 1: The letter says the statue is estimated to be over 150 feet tall! Just one of its fingers alone is 8 feet long. Its eye is nearly 3 feet wide, and its nose is almost 5 feet long.

GOVERNMENT WORKER 2: That's huge. How are we going to get that statue here from France? We need help! Let's talk with someone in the Shipping Department.

[Enter Shipping Department Worker.]

 From *Hello Hi-Lo: Readers Theatre Math* by Jeff Sanders and Nancy I. Sanders. Santa Barbara, CA: Libraries Unlimited. Copyright © 2010.

SHIPPING DEPARTMENT
WORKER: I'll help you, but hurry up. I don't have much time. I'm leaving for a trip in just a few moments and won't be back for three months. You say that the Statue of Liberty is estimated to be over 150 feet tall?

GOVERNMENT
WORKER 1: That's what the letter says. Its right arm alone is 42 feet long.

GOVERNMENT
WORKER 2: It's huge! How are we going to get it here from France? You can't just put a big statue like that on a boat. You can't ship it all in one piece.

SHIPPING DEPARTMENT
WORKER: You're right. We'll have to divide it into pieces and pack each piece in its own crate. If we do it that way and pack everything carefully, all the crates can be put on a ship to sail from France to America.

GOVERNMENT
WORKER 1: I recommend starting the paperwork to order those crates right away.

GOVERNMENT
WORKER 2: We can't wait until you're back from your trip. It might not arrive here in time for the celebration.

SHIPPING DEPARTMENT
WORKER: What else does the letter say?

GOVERNMENT
WORKER 1: The letter has an inventory saying that there are 16 pieces for the base and 56 pieces for the shoulders. Also, there are 37 pieces for the feet and 9 pieces for the book.

GOVERNMENT
WORKER 2: Don't forget! The letter says there are 96 pieces for the statue's robe.

SHIPPING DEPARTMENT WORKER: I don't have time to add all those numbers exactly. An estimate should be good enough. Let's round all those numbers and add them quickly so I can place the order for the number of crates right away before I leave on my trip.

GOVERNMENT WORKER 1: If we round each number to the nearest 10, we can estimate the sum of all the numbers quite easily.

GOVERNMENT WORKER 2: That would be 20 for the base and 60 for the shoulders. That's a total of 80 crates so far. Plus we have 40 pieces for the feet and 10 pieces for the book. Now we're up to 130 crates.

GOVERNMENT WORKER 1: And if we round 96 up to 100, we can add that to 130. That's an estimated total sum of 230 crates.

GOVERNMENT WORKER 2: I think that's everything. We didn't forget a single piece.

SHIPPING DEPARTMENT WORKER: That sounds like a reasonable estimate to give us enough crates to ship the entire statue on one boat. I'll place the order right away for 230 crates.

[Exit Shipping Department Worker. Enter Postal Worker.]

POSTAL WORKER: Special delivery! Another letter just arrived from France and it's marked extremely urgent. Here you are.

[Exit Postal Worker.]

GOVERNMENT WORKER 1: Oh no! Look here! This letter also explains that first France has to raise enough money so they can build the statue.

GOVERNMENT WORKER 2: That's going to be a lot of money. I wonder where they'll get enough money to build a statue that big?

GOVERNMENT
WORKER 1: But there's more! This letter says that America has to help pay for it, too! We have to get enough money to build a pedestal to put the statue on.

GOVERNMENT
WORKER 2: This is terrible. How can we pay for something that big? We need help. Who should we talk with about this?

GOVERNMENT
WORKER 1: We better talk with someone in the Finance Department.

[Enter Finance Department Worker.]

FINANCE
DEPARTMENT
WORKER: How may I help you today?

GOVERNMENT
WORKER 1: We just got a letter from France saying we have to get enough money to build a giant colossal pedestal for the Statue of Liberty.

GOVERNMENT
WORKER 2: I don't think we can get all that money.

FINANCE
DEPARTMENT
WORKER: I can help you. We do this kind of thing all the time. It's our job. You've come to the right place.

GOVERNMENT
WORKER 1: What should we do? How can we even attempt to raise that colossal amount of money?

GOVERNMENT
WORKER 2: We don't even know where to start.

FINANCE
DEPARTMENT
WORKER: Let's start at the beginning. First tell me how much money you think you will need. Then I can give you ideas about how to get it. It will all add up. It always does.

GOVERNMENT WORKER 1:	I don't know how much a thing like this would cost. We'll have to pay for the price of the materials for the pedestal, but I have no idea what that would be.
GOVERNMENT WORKER 2:	And we'll have to pay for the workers to build it, too. Don't forget to add that in.
FINANCE DEPARTMENT WORKER:	I'll call a builder I know. I'll ask him for numbers. He'll give me an honest quote.

[Enter Builder.]

BUILDER:	Thanks for giving me a call. For a job this big, it will cost $124,965.87 for materials. The charge for labor will be $125,274.63.
FINANCE DEPARTMENT WORKER:	That's good to know. Now let's round those numbers. That will make it easier to work with.
BUILDER:	Okay. We can use a number line or we can use the rules for rounding to round the numbers. What's your preference?
FINANCE DEPARTMENT WORKER:	Let's just use the rules. Those are pretty fast. That will help us get the right numbers.
BUILDER:	Okay. Since we're following the rules for rounding, first we should determine which place we want to round to.
FINANCE DEPARTMENT WORKER:	Let's round to the nearest ten thousand.
BUILDER:	Great. Grab a pencil and mark that number by either circling it or drawing a line underneath it. Now let's look at the digit to the right. If it's less than 5, don't change the digit that you marked. If it's 5 or greater than 5, round up the digit you marked. Then change all the digits to the right to zeroes.

74

GOVERNMENT WORKER 1: That will give us $125,000.00 for the materials and $125,000.00 for the labor. That's a total of $250,000.00!

GOVERNMENT WORKER 2: This is terrible! How will we ever find that much money? It's impossible!

FINANCE DEPARTMENT WORKER: Not really. We can have art shows. We can have plays. We can even have prize fights. We'll raise the money you need. I'll get started on it right away.

[Exit Finance Department Worker and Builder. Enter Postal Worker.]

POSTAL WORKER: Special delivery!

GOVERNMENT WORKER 1: Oh no! Not another special delivery letter from France!

POSTAL WORKER: Actually, it's not. This time I have bags and bags filled with letters from all sorts of people in America. Everyone knows the news about our surprise from France. There's even a noisy crowd of people outside your door.

[Exit Postal Worker.]

GOVERNMENT WORKER 2: Why is there a crowd outside our door? What do they want?

CROWD: We've heard the news about the statue from France, and we want to celebrate! We want to have fun! We want cake and ice cream and balloons. We want to be there when the statue is all finished. We want to have a party!

GOVERNMENT WORKER 1: But how many people are coming to the celebration?

GOVERNMENT WORKER 2: How much food will we have to get?

CROWD: We intend to invite our cousins. We intend to invite our aunts and uncles.

GOVERNMENT
WORKER 1: We better get ready for all these humongous crowds of people to arrive.

GOVERNMENT
WORKER 2: We better make sure we order enough cake and ice cream.

CROWD: We want to invite our neighbors. We want to invite our friends. We want to invite everyone we know, even the president of the United States!

GOVERNMENT
WORKER 1: This sounds like it will be a colossal party!

GOVERNMENT
WORKER 2: This is terrible! How are we ever going to figure out much food we'll need to feed all those people? How are we ever going to figure out how much money all this will cost?

GOVERNMENT
WORKER 1: I know! We'll ask everyone to let us know how many people they are inviting. Then we'll round the numbers so it will be easy to add. And then we'll estimate the sum.

GOVERNMENT
WORKER 2: What a great idea! That will help a lot. We'll be prepared for the big day.

GOVERNMENT
WORKER 1: Estimating really helps when we're working with such big numbers. But after the party's over, I think we'll need a colossal vacation. How many days do you estimate it will take us to recover from all this planning?

GOVERNMENT
WORKER 2: I think two weeks in France will be perfect. Let's get our tickets now. Come on! Let's go talk with the Travel Department right away!

POSSIBLE EXTENSIONS

1. Learn all about the Statue of Liberty by visiting the official site of the National Park Service at www.nps.gov/stli. As a class, review the statistics as well as the history of the Statue of Liberty. According to their skill level, invite students to write original word problems using statistics about the statue that give them practice rounding numbers.

2. Have students use number lines to show why the government workers in this fictitious account estimated that the shipping department should order 230 crates to ship the Statue of Liberty to America.

3. Explore other colossal landmarks with your students, such as the Space Needle, the St. Louis Gateway Arch, the Pyramids, and the Great Wall of China. Work with students to round numbers and estimate statistics about these landmarks. When they're finished, invite students to write original readers theatre plays about these landmarks using the numbers and math skills they practiced together. Allow time for groups of students to perform these plays for the class.

4. Assign students to look in the news for current events stories in which reporters estimated the numbers involved. Have them write short articles about the current event and explain why they think the news reports rounded or estimated these numbers.

CHAPTER 10

Detective Smart, Private Eye (Positive and Negative Numbers)

STAGING: Detective Smart may stand in the center of the stage. Seat the bank teller at the far left of the stage. The penguins may sit across the back of the stage. The polar bears are seated to the far right. Big Foot is seated near the front right of the stage. As the play progresses, Detective Smart may walk around the stage to speak with witnesses and the various suspects.

CHARACTERS

Detective Smart	Polar Bears 1 and 2
Bank Teller	Big Foot
Penguins	

```
                        Penguins
              X   X   X   X   X   X   X   X


                                              Polar
                                            Bears 1, 2
                                              X   X

        Bank Teller     Detective Smart
            X                 X             Big Foot
                                               X
```

Detective Smart, Private Eye

Scene 1: Florida National Bank, in Florida

DETECTIVE SMART: Detective Smart here. I'm a private eye. I specialize in solving the tough cases. Today it's a case of positives and negatives. The clues are baffling.

BANK TELLER: It was awful. The day started out cold and windy. As everyone in town could testify, there was ice on the street.

DETECTIVE SMART: Stick to the facts. Were you positive there was ice? Did you see ice here in the sunshine state?

BANK TELLER: Yes! I slipped on it as I walked up to the bank. It was so cold I had to wear mittens and a hat. Even after I buttoned my coat, the wind cut through me like a knife.

DETECTIVE SMART: The report says it was 10 degrees below zero. That's cold. On a frigid day like that, anything can happen. Start at the beginning and tell us all the positive and negative numbers. I'll write everything down.

BANK TELLER: I opened the bank as usual. Mrs. Frank came in and withdrew $100. That's how much she always takes. She uses it to buy food.

DETECTIVE SMART: Did you notice anything unusual happening?

BANK TELLER: Yes! It got so cold! In just a few minutes, my hands were as cold as ice. My nose turned blue. My feet felt like they were frozen. All in all, I felt like an ice cube frozen inside a freezer.

DETECTIVE SMART: The report says it dropped to 27 degrees below zero. That's quite a negative temperature on a thermometer. Is that when it happened?

BANK TELLER: Yes! The doors flew open. The lights went dark, and a stranger walked into the bank. He took all our money. Then he ran out the door.

DETECTIVE SMART: The report says he got away with three million dollars. Did you get a description? Did anyone see the thief?

BANK TELLER:	How could we? It was dark! All I know is that it was cold. How will we ever catch the thief?
DETECTIVE SMART:	Do the math. No ordinary thief works in that kind of cold in such negative temperatures. It was either a penguin, a polar bear, or Big Foot.

Scene 2: The South Pole

DETECTIVE SMART:	I'm hard on the trail of the thief. I'm here at the South Pole looking for Max the Penguin. He's no ordinary thief. He's known for hanging out with a rough crowd down here at the bottom of the world. His favorite place is in the Valley of the Penguins. It's 3,516 feet below sea level.
PENGUINS:	Who are you? And what are you doing down here? Nobody travels to this place unless they have some business to take care of.
DETECTIVE SMART:	I'm Detective Smart, Private Eye. Here's my card.
PENGUINS:	So we see your card. What's your business? You better have a genuine excuse for being here.
DETECTIVE SMART:	I'm on the lookout for Max the Penguin. Have you seen him?
PENGUINS:	Max hasn't been in these parts for months. They say he got in a bad deal with a seal. Or maybe it was a walrus. You get the picture. Whatever trouble he got himself into, they ran him out of town.
DETECTIVE SMART:	You're positive he hasn't been here where the temperatures are as negative as 94 degrees below zero? It's worth 10 grand to anyone who can give me a clue of absolute value.
PENGUINS:	Keep your money. We haven't seen him. Now vanish before we make you disappear.
DETECTIVE SMART:	My boat left and won't be back until spring.
PENGUINS:	So who needs a boat? We've got a fancy rocket ship with engines so powerful you'll wonder where we got them. We can blast you anywhere on this round globe that you want to go. We can even blast you clear to the North Pole.

DETECTIVE SMART:	I'll take it. When does it leave?
PENGUINS:	Just climb on board and the countdown begins. Launch time minus 5 minutes. Minus 4 minutes. Minus 3 minutes. Minus 2 minutes. Minus 1 minute. Blast off!

Scene 3: The North Pole

DETECTIVE SMART:	I'm looking for Powa the Polar Bear. Has anyone seen him anywhere up here in the Arctic Circle?
POLAR BEAR 1:	I know him. My pal and I just saw him this morning. He was eating breakfast at Guy's Dump. It's got the best fish pancakes on this side of the iceberg.
POLAR BEAR 2:	He lives around here. He's one of the wealthiest wise cracks who ever migrated to this part of town. What do you want with him?
DETECTIVE SMART:	I'm hot on the trail of a thief who stole three million dollars this morning. He worked in weather so cold it could snap a frozen sardine in half.
POLAR BEAR 1:	How cold is that?
DETECTIVE SMART:	It was 27 degrees below zero.
POLAR BEAR 2:	That bit of reporting doesn't sound like Powa the Polar Bear is the one you're looking for.
POLAR BEAR 1:	He's gone soft. He doesn't work in the cold like he used to. He started playing the stock markets. After he made some money, he gave up the tough life.
POLAR BEAR 2:	Now he stays indoors when the thermometer shows negative numbers. Besides, we saw him at breakfast.
POLAR BEAR 1:	That's right. He was at Guy's Dump. He eats breakfast there every morning.
POLAR BEAR 2:	The only place you'll see him after breakfast is the stock market. He watches the increases and decreases in stocks like he's watching for a seal on the ice.
DETECTIVE SMART:	If you're positive, then I'll take your word. While I'm in the area, I'll look up my next suspect. Have either of you seen Big Foot?
POLAR BEAR 1:	We don't hang out with that kind of crowd. He's too cold for us.

POLAR BEAR 2:	If you want to find Big Foot as your next suspect, you'll have to look on the other side of the iceberg.
DETECTIVE SMART:	Thanks. I'll do that. I'm just looking for clues with an absolute value.

Scene 4: The Other Side of the Iceberg

DETECTIVE SMART:	They said I would find you here where the days are as dark as the company you keep.
BIG FOOT:	So? What are you trying to say? What do you want with me?
DETECTIVE SMART:	The North Pole Bank says you made a deposit of three million dollars just after lunch.
BIG FOOT:	So? I got paid. Everyone gets paid. Why should I be any different?
DETECTIVE SMART:	Nobody gets a paycheck worth three million dollars. Where were you this morning?
BIG FOOT:	I was over at Guy's Dump. I had three fish pancakes. It was 8 degrees below zero.
DETECTIVE SMART:	I've got two polar bears who say you weren't there. Don't give me negative numbers like that or I'll throw the book at you.
BIG FOOT:	So where do you say I was?
DETECTIVE SMART:	I say you were at a different bank this morning. A bank that normally has sunny skies. A bank that got so cold it felt like everything turned to ice. It was 27 degrees below zero.
BIG FOOT:	Who says you can prove it?
DETECTIVE SMART:	I say that anyone who works in those negative temperatures has to be either a penguin, a polar bear, or Big Foot.
BIG FOOT:	So? Why do you think it's me?
DETECTIVE:	I talked with the penguins. Max the Penguin hasn't been seen for months. I found the polar bears. Powa the Polar Bear has gone soft. He doesn't work in the cold anymore. Three million dollars in the North Pole Bank says it's you.

BIG FOOT: All right. All right. I did it. If I come along, what will I have to do?

DETECTIVE SMART: With a record like yours, I'd say it will be at least three years cooking fish pancakes at Guy's Dump. But if you turn yourself in and meet me at the station in an hour, I'll make sure to get you a break.

BIG FOOT: I'll do it! I'll do it! Just don't make me stand on my big feet all day. With feet this big, they get tired fast. Give me a desk job instead. I'll give back the three million to the bank lady with the blue nose if you do.

DETECTIVE SMART: It's a deal. Case closed. I'm a private eye. I specialize in solving the tough cases. Today it was simply a matter of positives and negatives.

POSSIBLE EXTENSIONS

1. Track your weather and compare it with Antarctica's. Set up an outdoor thermometer near your classroom to track the temperature in your area over the course of this lesson. Each day, graph the temperature on a number line. Simultaneously on a second number line, track the temperature each day at the South Pole by visiting the Web site www.antarcticconnection.com/antarctic/weather/index.shtml. Practice using positive and negative numbers as you compare each day's readings in both parts of the world.

2. For a variety of cross-curricular activities as well as printable worksheets for students to use when learning how to add and subtract positive and negative integers while working with thermometers, visit the Web site www.enchantedlearning.com/science/temperature/.

3. Invite students to play a fast-paced game for real-world experience working with positive and negative integers. This educational program gives students the chance to invest a hypothetical $100,000 in an online portfolio. Learn more about how your class can sharpen math skills as well as key economic and financial concepts by exploring the Stock Market Game at www.stockmarketgame.org/.

4. Build a model rocket with your students. Before it is launched, discuss how positive and negative numbers are used to measure the time before and after launching a rocket. Launch the rocket together. After the exciting event is over, ask students to write a report in their journals about what happened during the 10 seconds of the countdown and in the 10 seconds immediately after takeoff. Have them draw a number line in their journals as a reference to the timings in their reports.

5. Play Batter Up with your class. This outdoor game reinforces skills using positive and negative numbers. Divide students into small groups of four to nine players, with no more than nine in one group. To play the game, go outside on a large playing field. Each group plays its own game of Batter Up. Each group needs one tennis ball and one racquet ball racquet. Each group has a scorekeeper who needs a clipboard, pen, and paper.

    To play the game, one person is the batter. One person is the scorekeeper and will mark down each player's score as the game is played. The rest of the players are in the outfield. The batter tosses the ball in the air and hits it to the outfield. Each player is responsible for keeping his or her own score. At the end of the game, the scores should be checked for accuracy with the scorekeeper. Here are the guidelines for scoring points:

    -   If a player catches a fly ball, it's 100 points.
    -   If a player catches a fly ball, but drops it, it's –100 points.
    -   If the ball bounces off one person and then the next person catches it, the player who catches the ball scores 100 points. If that person drops the ball, it's –100 points.
    -   If the ball bounces on the ground one time and then a player catches it, it's 75 points. It's –75 points if that player drops it.
    -   If the ball bounces on the ground two times and then a player catches it, it's 50 points. It's –50 points if that player drops it.
    -   If the ball bounces three or more times or rolls on the ground, and then a player catches it, it's 25 points. It's –25 points if that player drops it.
    -   The last player to touch the ball earns the points. If the ball stops dead before someone catches it, 0 points are earned.

- The first person to get 200 points goes up to bat, and everyone's score goes back to 0. Or, if the game is taking too long, after five minutes the player with the highest score goes up to bat, and everyone's score goes back to 0.

- The last batter then becomes the new scorekeeper.

- Nobody gets two turns to bat. If someone gets the points to go up to bat more than once, that person picks someone else to bat in his or her place.

- Play until every player has a turn at bat.

CHAPTER 11

The Silly History of Transportation: Otherwise Known as the "Invention" of Points, Lines, and Planes (Points, Lines, and Planes)

STAGING: Seat the narrator at the far left front of the stage. Group the caveman family standing together in the center front of the stage. The rest of the characters should wait off-stage. The caveman family should exit the stage when they are done speaking. Then the Ice Age Teens will come on stage and stand in the front center to speak. After their turn is finished and they exit the stage, the Roman Officer and Soldiers should enter and stand in the center front of the stage. They will exit when they are done speaking. The two engineers should then walk on stage and stand together in the center to talk for their turn.

CHARACTERS

Narrator	Ice Age Teens 1 and 2
Caveman Kids 1 and 2	Roman Officer
Caveman Mom	Roman Soldiers
Caveman Dad	Engineers 1 and 2

```
┌─────────────────────────────────────────────────────────┐
│                                                          │
│                                                          │
│       Caveman      Caveman     Caveman     Caveman        │
│        Kid 1        Kid 2        Dad         Mom          │
│          X            X           X           X           │
│                                                          │
│   Narrator                                                │
│      X                                                    │
│                                                          │
└─────────────────────────────────────────────────────────┘
```

The Silly History of Transportation

NARRATOR: This is a silly story about the history of transportation. Some people say it probably started in the very beginning when cavemen lived in caves. But I think that's silly.

CAVEMAN KID 1: I'm tired of living in caves. Would there be any way that we could go outside once in awhile?

CAVEMAN KID 2: Can we visit someone? We've heard there are people who live in the cave across the valley, but we've never even met them.

CAVEMAN DAD: Never! There are woolly mammoths out there! And what about all those ferocious saber-toothed tigers?

CAVEMAN MOM: But dear, think of the children. It really would be good for them to go outside and play. I think they're old enough to go across the valley.

CAVEMAN KIDS 1 AND 2: Ple-e-ease?

CAVEMAN DAD: Well, okay. But do you really think someone can travel all the way to the opposite side of the valley? Nobody has ever gone that far before.

CAVEMAN KID 1: Last night I thought about what we could do to get there. First I'll stand on a spot right outside our door. I'll call that Point A. Then I'll hop to another spot. That will be Point B.

CAVEMAN KID 2: Fantastic idea! We can hop from point to point all the way to the cave across the valley.

CAVEMAN DAD: But do you think it's a safe way to get around? I could guard you with my spear and perhaps light a fire if any dangerous animal gets too close.

From *Hello Hi-Lo: Readers Theatre Math* by Jeff Sanders and Nancy I. Sanders. Santa Barbara, CA: Libraries Unlimited. Copyright © 2010.

CAVEMAN MOM: That sounds wonderful. If you wait a minute, I'll put on my brand new sloth fur coat and come along. We can all hop from point to point. We'll be there in no time.

NARRATOR: And so it was that the point was invented. Soon cave men all over the valley could be seen hopping from point to point to get from one cave to another. This went on for years until one day during the Ice Age . . .

ICE AGE TEEN 1: Hey, what do you have there? It looks big and round. It's almost like a sphere, but it's totally not because it's flat on both sides.

ICE AGE TEEN 2: I call this a wheel. It's my new invention.

ICE AGE TEEN 1: How does it work? And what do you use it for? I've never seen anything like it before.

ICE AGE TEEN 2: I put two wheels together and added a seat. I call it a bike. I can sit on my bike and ride it from point to point. Now I don't have to hop through the ice and snow all the way across the valley. I can just ride in a straight line.

ICE AGE TEEN 1: Line? What's a line? I've never heard anyone say a fantastic word like that before.

ICE AGE TEEN 2: A line goes through two points. It's another one of my inventions. A line can go on and on in both directions and never stop.

ICE AGE TEEN 1: I get it. What a great way to get around. May I join your team? We could start a business making these bikes. I bet all our friends will buy one so they can ride in a straight line from their place to someone else's. We'll make millions of dollars!

ICE AGE TEEN 2: Sure! You can be in charge of sales. Soon we'll be selling bikes to everyone on the planet. That will give me money to work on my next invention.

ICE AGE TEEN 1: What's your next invention?

ICE AGE TEEN 2: I want to invent a machine to melt all this ice. Then we can really get around! Maybe one day we'll even ride a bike in a straight line out of our valley. We'll see the world!

NARRATOR:	With the invention of the line, transportation was never the same. Soon there were so many lines drawn all over the place that bikes were crashing into each other at an alarming rate. Until one day, during the Roman Empire . . .
ROMAN OFFICER:	This is ridiculous! There are lines everywhere! Who invented all these lines, anyway? They go in whichever direction, and who knows where they're going? Something has to be done.
ROMAN SOLDIERS:	What would you like us to do about this terrible problem?
ROMAN OFFICER:	First, mark two parallel lines going from east to west. These lines will always be the same distance apart. Then build two roads along those two parallel lines. One road will be for our famous horses and the other road will be for our beautiful parades.
ROMAN SOLDIERS:	That's a good idea. But sometimes people want to go north or south. What should we do if we need roads going in a different direction?
ROMAN OFFICER:	Mark lines that intersect the first. If you want perpendicular lines, you can make them intersect at right angles. Otherwise, the lines can intersect at whatever angles you want. After all the lines are drawn, build roads on top of them.
ROMAN SOLDIERS:	We'll get started right away. But first we have a question. Some people just want to start at one point and go in one direction. Other people like to start at one point and end at another point. What should we do about that?
ROMAN OFFICER:	Good point. I know what you can do. Draw line segments, too. A line segment is only part of a line. It has two endpoints. You can also draw rays. A ray is a line that starts at one point and then goes on in one direction. After you've drawn all these lines, build roads on top of them. We'll have the best roads built in the entire history of transportation!

NARRATOR: True to the officer's prediction, the Romans designed and built roads all over their empire. They rode their horses everywhere, from the smallest village to the largest city of all, Rome! This went on for ages, until one day, two brothers invented something that could lift people up into the air so they could fly like a bird from one place to the next.

ENGINEER 1: What do they call that new invention those two famous brothers came up with?

ENGINEER 2: A plane. It's a fantastic machine! The only problem with it, though, is that it doesn't make very safe landings.

ENGINEER 1: We'll fix that. That's what they hired us for. It's our job to come up with a way for these brand new planes to land quickly and easily.

ENGINEER 2: Do you have any ideas about where we should start?

ENGINEER 1: First of all, we need a really flat surface. Every time those brothers tried to land their plane on a hill or a mountain, it crashed.

ENGINEER 2: Have you noticed we're standing right now in a field that is really flat? This could be the perfect place to have the planes land.

ENGINEER 1: You're right! Look—here is a point where one plane could land. And over there is another point. And look! There's a third point over there. This field is so flat it has points all over the place where one of these brand new planes can safely land.

ENGINEER 2: What should we call this flat surface? It's got to have the right name so we can tell those two inventor brothers where to land their plane.

ENGINEER 1: Let's call this flat surface a plane! That way nobody will get mixed-up or confused. The plane can land on a plane. Everyone will remember that.

ENGINEER 2: Right. From now on a plane will be a flat surface with at least three points on it that aren't all in a straight line. It's the perfect spot for a plane to land.

NARRATOR: And there you have it. You've just heard the silly history of transportation. Or, as some people like to call it, the invention of points, lines, and planes.

POSSIBLE EXTENSIONS

1. Play Geometry Bingo with your class. On a piece of typing paper, prepare a blank 5-by-5-inch grid to resemble a standard Bingo card. In the center square, write "Free Space." At the top of each column, instead of writing B-I-N-G-O, write in this order: "Point," "Line," "Segment," "Ray," and "Plane." (Note: Adjust headings according to the skill level of your students. For instance, if you're only studying points and lines, write at the top of each column in this order: "Point 1," "Point 2," "Line 1," "Line 2," "Segment".)

    Photocopy the Geometry Bingo card and distribute one copy to each student. On the board or on a bulletin board, list different possible combinations of symbols for points, lines, segments, rays, and planes with 15 geometric figures under each heading. Direct students to then randomly choose geometric figures from each column to write in the corresponding columns on their own Bingo cards until the cards are full. Have students each tear or cut a piece of red construction paper into one-inch pieces to use as markers for their boards. Each player needs 25 markers.

    Play the game according to the rules of regular Bingo. Call out different geometric figures from the board, such as point *A*, line *DC*, or line segment *VT*. Mark off each symbol that you call with a sticky note or some other method that is not permanent (so you may play the game more than once). The winner is the first player or players to complete a predetermined pattern on their boards, such as a line (vertical, horizontal, or diagonal) or a full house (all the squares are covered).

2. Play a game of Geometric Concentration. Using three blank index cards, write one matching set of a symbol, written name, and image of a geometric figure. For instance, one card could have the written name Point *B*. The second card would have the symbol for Point *B*. The third card would have the picture of Point *B*. Repeat for seven more sets of matching cards, each with a different geometric figure. There will be a total of 24 cards. (Or you may make more sets for older students.)

    To play the game, two students shuffle the cards and place them facedown one-by-one and all spread out. The first player flips over three cards, trying to find a three-way match. If the three cards do not match, they are turned back over in their place and the other player takes a turn. If the cards are a match, that player takes another turn. Play continues until all the matches are found.

3. Turn math into an art lesson to reinforce kinesthetic learning. Study a famous artist or painting that uses geometric shapes and figures. For instance, the painting style pointillism uses small dots or points of color to create a larger image. After viewing and discussing a painting, invite students to create their own pieces of art either using pointillism or incorporating the geometric figures you are studying into their paintings or drawings.

4. Draw a Venn diagram on the board. Compare and contrast two geometric figures, such as a line and a line segment, while completing the Venn diagram. Next instruct students to draw a Venn diagram and complete it, comparing and contrasting two more geometric figures such as a point and a ray. Discuss results.

CHAPTER 12

Super Girl (Angles)

STAGING: Seat the narrator at the far left front of the stage and the doctor at the far right front. Group the neighbors sitting near the right of the stage, behind the doctor. In center stage, seat Super Dad and Super Mom, with Super Girl sitting between them.

CHARACTERS

Narrator	Super Girl
Super Mom	Neighbors
Super Dad	Doctor

Neighbors
Super Dad   Super Girl   Super Mom   X   X   X
X   X   X   X   X

Narrator   Doctor
X   X

Super Girl

NARRATOR: Our story begins in a small town. A husband and wife lived there on an ordinary street. But they were not like everyone else. They were superheroes! One day they had a little baby girl. They named her Super Girl.

SUPER DAD: Oh, isn't she cute? Even her little smile is adorable. Look at her cute little teeny tiny fingers and toes. And she's even got arms of steel. Before we know it, she'll be lifting up cars and trucks. She's such a cute baby!

SUPER MOM: She's got your X-ray vision, beautiful blue eyes. Soon she'll be able to see through walls. And what a cute laugh she has! It reminds me of yours. She's Daddy's little girl.

NARRATOR: Super Dad and Super Mom heard a knock on their door. It was the neighbors.

NEIGHBORS: Oh, what a cute little baby girl you have! Enjoy every minute you can with her. Before you know it, she'll be all grown up and you'll wonder where the years have flown.

NARRATOR: Super Dad and Super Mom took good care of their little baby. One day, she got her very first tooth.

SUPER DAD: Just look at that new little white tooth in her rosy red mouth. What a cute little white tooth she has! Isn't she adorable?

SUPER MOM: Now that her first tooth grew in, we can start to feed her real food she can chew. Won't that be simply wonderful?

SUPER GIRL: Mama! Dad-dad! May I have pizza, please?

SUPER DAD: Oh, isn't that cute! She just pronounced her very first words, and the first thing she's asking for is a piece of my favorite food. Pizza!

SUPER MOM: Don't you think she's a little too young for pizza? Shouldn't we wait to feed her a slice of pizza until she's at least a few years older?

 From *Hello Hi-Lo: Readers Theatre Math* by Jeff Sanders and Nancy I. Sanders. Santa Barbara, CA: Libraries Unlimited. Copyright © 2010.

SUPER DAD:	Not if we just give her a cute little piece.
SUPER MOM:	Okay. I'll cut a cute, tiny little triangle of pizza for her to eat.
SUPER DAD:	You cut that piece of pizza with such acute, tiny little angles that it's small enough for our cute little girl to eat.
SUPER MOM:	We can cut all her food into cute little triangles.
SUPER DAD:	Each piece can be an adorable triangle with acute, tiny little angles. I'll cut her a cute, tiny piece of pie with acute, tiny little angles. I'll cut her a cute, tiny piece of cake with acute, tiny little angles.
SUPER MOM:	Do you think with just one tooth our little girl is ready for pieces of pie and pieces of cake, too?
SUPER GIRL:	Mama. Dad-dad. I love pie and cake, and I love pizza, too! And each piece is so cute.
NARRATOR:	Just then, Super Dad and Super Mom heard a knock on their door. It was the neighbors.
NEIGHBORS:	It's been awhile since we've seen your cute little girl. She's so cute, but we're worried about how she's doing these days. She doesn't seem to be growing and developing like she should be.
SUPER DAD:	Are you sure? Are you absolutely certain?
NEIGHBORS:	Has she been able to lift a car yet with her cute little finger? Has she been able to see through a wall yet with her cute, X-ray vision, beautiful blue eyes?
SUPER MOM:	No. We haven't seen any evidence of her super powers just yet.
NEIGHBORS:	See what we mean? If she was our cute little girl, we'd hurry and take her to see the doctor right away.
NARRATOR:	They quickly took their cute little girl to see the best doctor in town.
DOCTOR:	I've examined your cute little girl thoroughly. It seems that she is suffering from a case of acute angles.
SUPER MOM:	Oh, Doctor, is it serious? What should we do?

DOCTOR: This condition isn't serious yet. But you must start feeding her bigger portions. If she wants pizza, it's obvious that you'll need to cut her pieces of pizza with big, obtuse angles.

SUPER DAD: What if she wants pie or cake? Is it healthy to give her pieces of pie and cake cut with big, obtuse angles, too?

DOCTOR: Obviously! And it's obvious that the bigger the angle, the better. Obtuse angles are the best for a little superhero in her condition. Give her generous portions so she'll really start to grow.

NARRATOR: Super Dad and Super Mom hurried home. They gave their little girl the biggest pieces of pizza that they could cut. They gave their little girl the biggest pieces of pie and cake that they could cut.

SUPER DAD: Here you are, Super Girl! This is obviously the biggest obtuse angle I could cut this piece of pizza without giving you half of it.

SUPER GIRL: Thanks, Super Dad. I like eating big pieces of pizza, so this looks great. It's nearly half a pizza! Eating this large a piece of pizza will make me really strong.

SUPER MOM: After you eat, dear, will you please pick up all of your toys and put them away in your room?

SUPER GIRL: Sure, Mom. I'll pick up our piano, too. Would you like it in the family room or the living room?

SUPER MOM: Oh, this is wonderful! Please put it in the family room. It's obviously the best place suited for it.

SUPER DAD: And while you're helping us move the furniture, could you pick up our couch and put it in the living room? It's the obvious spot for it now that the piano isn't there.

SUPER GIRL: Of course! I can pick up anything and move it anywhere you want. Would you like me to pick up the refrigerator? I can move it, too.

SUPER MOM: No, I don't think so. The obvious place to keep it is in the kitchen. The refrigerator can stay where it is.

SUPER GIRL: I'm done picking up my toys now, so may I go outside and play in the front yard?

SUPER DAD: Yes, but be sure to stay inside our fence and not run out into the road. Don't forget that there's a busy intersection in front of our house with cars, trucks, and other vehicles that drive past each day.

NARRATOR: Super Girl went outside to play. Soon, however, Super Dad and Super Mom heard a knock on their door. It was the neighbors.

NEIGHBORS: Have you seen your little girl today? She's out in your front yard pulling your trees out of the ground! What amazing strength she has! It's obvious you've been feeding her too much. It's obvious you're using big, obtuse angles to cut her food.

NARRATOR: Super Dad and Super Mom went outside to look.

SUPER GIRL: Look, everyone! I can pull out this giant oak tree with just one finger. I can lift three cars and six trucks over my head. I can see deep under the ground with my X-ray vision. I can see all the way to China on the opposite side of the world!

NEIGHBORS: See what we mean? It's obvious you've been feeding her too much. If she was our little girl, we'd hurry and take her to see the doctor right away.

NARRATOR: Super Dad and Super Mom took Super Girl to see the doctor.

DOCTOR: I've examined your little girl thoroughly. It's obvious that she is suffering from a case of obtuse angles.

SUPER MOM: Oh, Doctor, is it serious? What should we do?

DOCTOR: This condition isn't serious yet. But you must start feeding her portions that are just right. No more acute angles and no more obtuse angles. Only right angles will do.

SUPER DAD: But Doctor, how can we be expected to know what the right angle is when she wants a piece of pizza? How will we know the right angle to use when we cut her a piece of cake or pie?

DOCTOR: Right angles are everywhere. The corner of a piece of paper is a right angle. The corner of a book is a right angle. The corner of a door is a right angle. Just find a right angle and use it as a perfect reference to cut all her foods with right angles.

SUPER GIRL: Does this mean that I can still see to China with my X-ray vision eyes? Will I be able to lift three cars? Will I be able to pick up six trucks?

DOCTOR: Of course not! Girls your age are not supposed to be that strong. Not even superheroes.

SUPER GIRL: But what will happen to me?

DOCTOR: You'll be able to lift one car, just like superheroes your age should be able to do. You'll be able to see through only one wall with your X-ray vision eyes instead of all the way through the middle of the earth. Just eat food cut into pieces with right angles. You'll be all right in no time.

SUPER MOM: Oh, thank you, Doctor! We'll go home right now and get right to work.

SUPER DAD: We'll make sure our little girl has all the right food so she'll grow up to be just right.

POSSIBLE EXTENSIONS

1. Invite students to play a game similar to Spoons. To prepare for the game, use blank index cards to make a card deck of 16 cards. On four of the cards, draw one right angle per card. Underneath write "Right Angle." On four other cards, draw one acute angle, one per card. Underneath write "Acute Angle." On four other cards, draw one obtuse angle, one per card. Underneath write "Obtuse Angle." On the last four cards, draw a circle, one per card. Divide the circle into four sections, one with a right angle, one with an obtuse angle, and two with acute angles. (The vertex of each angle should be in the center of the circle.

    Four players sit together around a table. Place three plastic spoons in the center of the table. The dealer shuffles cards and distributes them to the players so that each player has four cards. The goal of the game is to get four matching cards of all the same angle (or circle).

    The dealer chooses one card from her hand, says "Pass," and passes it to the player on her left. Each player likewise chooses one card from his deck and passes it simultaneously to his left.

    When a player has four matching cards, she should grab a spoon from the center of the table. Everyone must then try to grab a spoon. The player left without a spoon has lost the round and is given an "S."

    The cards are shuffled and the spoons are returned to the center of the table. Play continues. The first person to spell s-p-o-o-n-s loses the game.

2. Give students their choice of the following activities to complete:

    – Cut out models of acute, obtuse, and right angles from paper.

    – Draw pictures of acute, obtuse, and right angles.

    – Make a list of items in the room that have an acute, obtuse, or right angle.

    When they are finished, ask the class to share their work.

3. Create a bulletin board display of circles cut into segments that represent three different types of angles. To practice, first instruct students to each draw a circle and divide it into eight segments, each with an acute angle. Then have each one draw a circle and divide it into three segments, each with an obtuse angle. Finally, have each draw a third circle and divide it into four segments, each with a right angle. Ask students to check each other's work in pairs.

    Have students then choose various colors of construction paper to make a large model of one of their drawings, large enough to display on the bulletin board. Display the work on the bulletin board by grouping circles with similar angles together and labeling the angles.

4. Divide students into pairs. Instruct each student to draw two acute angles and two obtuse angles on a sheet of paper. Then have each student estimate each angle's measurement by degrees. Instruct students to write down their estimations next to each angle, along with their initials. Partners should then swap papers and write down their estimations with their initials next to each angle the partner drew. Direct the students to measure each angle with a protractor to determine whose estimation was closest.

CHAPTER 13

Out of This World Video Game (Percentages)

STAGING: Seat the four friends in the center of the stage. The narrator may be seated at the far left front of the stage. The princess, Tatumn, may be seated at the far right front of the stage. Seat the Catastrophic Clones on the right back of the stage.

CHARACTERS

Narrator

Friends 1, 2, 3, and 4

Catastrophic Clones

Tatumn (the princess)

```
                                              Catastrophic
                                                 Clones
                                              X  X  X  X
                                                X  X  X

         Friend 1    Friend 2    Friend 3    Friend 4
            X           X           X           X

                                                      Tatumn
                                                     (Princess)
   Narrator                                              X
      X
```

Out of This World Video Game

NARRATOR:	One day, four friends met as they were going home from school.
FRIEND 1:	Do you want to come over to my house today? I've got a great new video game, but it takes four players.
FRIEND 2:	This sounds like fun! When can we come over?
FRIEND 1:	Meet me at 6:00 at my house after dinner and homework.
FRIENDS 2, 3, AND 4:	Count us in. Let's go!
NARRATOR:	The four friends met that evening.
FRIEND 3:	This is going to be fun! This game is so new, it looks like you haven't even opened the package yet. It's called the Out of This World Video Game.
FRIEND 1:	Here are the directions. Do you want me to read them aloud?
FRIEND 2:	Sure, go ahead.
FRIEND 1:	The directions say this is a high-speed and dangerous role-playing action game in which anything can happen.
FRIEND 4:	It's not talking about real, intense danger, is it?
FRIEND 3:	Actually, it says we are all going to be *in* the game. It says there's actually a real, genuine princess to save.
FRIEND 4:	What exactly does this mean? What are these directions talking about?
FRIEND 2:	What does it mean by saying there's a real princess to save?
FRIEND 3:	These directions aren't making any sense at all.
FRIEND 1:	I think we should just get started and play the game. We'll figure it out.

FRIEND 4: Okay. That sounds like a good idea.

FRIEND 1: First we're going to pick the color of our game board. There's blue, green, red, or yellow. Then we're going to pick our version. There's medieval or sci fi. Then we have to pick our race.

FRIEND 2: Say we pick sci fi. What are the choices for race?

FRIEND 1: There's cyborg, intergalactic trash collector, robot, or space warrior. After that, we'll need to pick our specialties. We can be a singer, a runner, a medic, or a thief.

FRIEND 3: This sounds fantastic! Let's start to choose right away.

FRIEND 4: I guess I'll start. I'll pick the green game board. I want to be a cyborg. I like to sing so I'll be a singer.

FRIEND 2: I pick the red game board. I'll be a robot. I want to be a medic.

FRIEND 3: I pick yellow. I'll be a space warrior, and I want to be a runner. I'm on the track team so I like to run.

FRIEND 1: Give me the blue game board and make me an intergalactic trash collector. I'll be a thief.

FRIEND 4: For this first level, the directions say we have to escape from the Fire Planet. Each of us gets a spaceship to fly.

FRIEND 2: This sounds so cool!

FRIEND 3: On each level, each of our game boards is a 10-by-10 grid made up of 100 squares. Each square you fly through adds up. For instance, if you fly through 10 squares on your grid, you score 10 percent. If you fly through 25 squares, you score 25 percent.

FRIEND 2: How do we beat each level? We need to know how to get to the level where we have to save the princess.

FRIEND 1: Let me see. Oh, here the directions say that if one of us gets 100 percent of our game board covered before the clock runs down to zero, we win that level. If nobody gets 100 percent by the time the clock runs down, then the player with the highest percentage wins that level.

FRIEND 3: Wait! Look there on that page of the directions. It says that we each carry a bag to collect things that will help us achieve our goals.

FRIEND 2: What kind of things do the directions say we collect?

FRIEND 1: It says if we collect power orbs, we can keep them in our bag and use them as fuel for our spaceship when our fuel runs low.

FRIEND 4: We can also use them as energy to go faster if we use them right away.

FRIEND 1: There are other things to collect, too. It says there are photon clusters, tools, energy bundles, and computer chips.

FRIEND 3: I guess we can collect them in our bag or use them right away like we do in other games.

FRIEND 2: Let's hurry up and start. It's almost time for me to go home.

FRIEND 1: Wait! Did you notice how the instructions say that our ultimate goal is to save the princess on Level 3, where she's frozen in a block of ice? And we have to watch out for the Catastrophic Clones hiding along the way.

NARRATOR: Each player held a control pad. Suddenly they were inside the game! Each had on a helmet and space suit that matched the color of his or her game board. Each climbed in his or her spaceship and took off.

FRIEND 1: Wow! I'm actually flying my own spaceship. Since I'm an intergalactic trash collector, I think I'll fly through a few squares on my 10-by-10 grid and collect whatever I find. Look! Here's an ice ray laser and a wrench. I'll put them in my bag. They might come in handy later. And look! I've already flown through 10 percent of my blue game board. This is so easy.

FRIEND 2: I'm not too sure about this level. Everything is on fire. How are we supposed to fly our spaceships around? The mountains are burning. The rocks are burning. Even the lakes are burning. I'm flying very slowly. I've only flown through 5 percent of my red game board.

FRIEND 3: Hey! What's this? Behind one of the burning boulders on my yellow game board are a bunch of little guys. They all look the same. Hey! They jumped out at me! What should I do?

CATASTROPHIC CLONES: Stop! We're the Catastrophic Clones! You can't get past us! You'll never escape from the Fire Planet.

FRIEND 3: Help! If I stay right here because they're blocking my way, I'll never win this level. What should I do?

FRIEND 4: Look to your left. You've got an energy bundle. Grab it! Maybe it will give you a burst of energy so you can get past those nasty looking clones.

FRIEND 3: It worked! I got the energy bundle. I was able to zoom past those clones so fast they couldn't tell what was happening. I'm still zooming! I've flown through 50 percent of my grid already.

FRIEND 4: Oh no, the clones are here on my green game board, too!

CATASTROPHIC CLONES: We show up anywhere we want. Now we're blocking your way, and you can't get past us like your friend did, because you don't have an energy bundle to help you escape.

FRIEND 4: You're right! But I collected five computer chips and have them here in my bag. Since I'm a cyborg, I can program these computer chips to help me sing. La la la! Do re mi fa so la ti do.

CATASTROPHIC CLONES: Now you've done it! You've locked us in a cage of musical notes for 30 seconds. We're frozen in time and can't break free until this imaginary cage disappears.

FRIEND 4: Great! I'll fly right past you to safety. I'm zooming through 53 percent of my board. I'm zooming through 76 percent of my board. I'm zooming right past a burning asteroid! I'm zooming through 100 percent of my board. I won!

FRIENDS 1, 2, AND 3: Help! Help! Help!

FRIEND 4: What's wrong?

FRIEND 1: As soon as you flew through 100 percent of your game board, our Fire Planets started to explode.

FRIEND 2: Fly over to our game boards and rescue us before it's too late!

FRIEND 4: Hang on, everyone! I'll zoom over to your game boards and pick up each one of you in my spaceship!

NARRATOR: Soon everyone was safe on board the same spaceship.

FRIENDS 1, 2, AND 3: Thanks for picking us up! But now that we're all in your spaceship, what are we going to do?

FRIEND 4: We have a princess to save! She's on Level 3, so first we have to fly back to my green game board and try to win the second level.

FRIEND 1: This looks like a water planet. Your spaceship turned into a submarine. Now we're going underwater. The game board is still a 10-by-10 grid, but everything is underneath the water.

FRIEND 3: Hurry! Let's get through this level as fast as we can. We're already through 43 percent of the squares on the grid.

FRIEND 1: Watch out! There's something hiding in that underwater cave up ahead. Is it a shark? Is it an octopus?

CATASTROPHIC CLONES: No! We're here again! We're the Catastrophic Clones! This time we'll damage your submarine. You'll never get past us.

FRIEND 4: Help! Help! They threw a high-energy blast that damaged our engine. We can't go anywhere now.

FRIEND 1: Wait a minute. I'm an intergalactic trash collector, so I picked up a wrench on Level 1 and have it here in my collector's bag. I'll use this to fix the engine.

FRIEND 4: Great! Now the engine's fixed. Before they can do anything else, we'll zoom past that cave where those clones are hiding.

CATASTROPHIC
CLONES: Not so fast! Here's another energy blast coming your way. This time we're aiming for the rocket boosters. Kaboom!

FRIEND 4: Oh no! Now the rocket boosters are damaged beyond repair. What are we going to do?

FRIEND 2: I'm a robot, and my specialty is that I'm a medic. I'll plug into the rocket boosters. Then I'll fix the boosters. The ship will be working in no time.

FRIEND 1: This time we'll blast past those nasty clones and cover this entire game board before the clock runs down to zero.

FRIEND 4: Hurry! Time's almost up. We're zooming through 62 percent of the board. Now we've covered 85 percent of the board. Now 97 percent of the board is covered, with only two seconds to go.

FRIEND 3: We did it! We flew over 100 percent of the grid with only one second left on the clock. And now we've made it to Level 3. This is where we save the princess. Does anyone see her?

FRIEND 2: There she is! I see her in that ice palace. It looks like she's frozen in a block of ice.

FRIEND 1: Somehow, she looks familiar.

FRIEND 3: It's our friend, Tatumn! How did she get here inside this video game when we were the only people at your house?

FRIEND 1: I don't know, but we better do everything we can to rescue her from her prison of ice.

FRIEND 4: I don't know how we're going to save her. Our submarine has changed back into a spaceship. But this level is an ice planet. It's so cold that both our engine and our rocket boosters are in danger of freezing.

FRIEND 3: Oh no! Look behind that iceberg. There those little look-alike guys are again.

CATASTROPHIC
CLONES: We'll never let you past us, even if you try for a millennium. You'll never save the princess.

FRIEND 2: But we have to save the princess. She's our friend!

CATASTROPHIC CLONES: You'll never make it to the ice castle. The temperature is falling so fast you'll freeze before you fly through another square on the grid.

FRIEND 1: This time, I think they're right! We've only flown through 23 percent of the grid, and our engine is nearly frozen solid.

CATASTROPHIC CLONES: We know we're right. The only way for you to save yourselves is to get power orbs to melt the ice and give you enough fuel to fly through the rest of the game board.

FRIEND 2: I'll get off the spaceship and collect power orbs in my bag! I'll carry them back here to save us.

CATASTROPHIC CLONES: Not so fast! We already collected all the power orbs here on this level and have them hidden in our ice cave. You'll never be able to escape! You'll never be able to save the princess!

FRIEND 1: I know! Since I'm a thief, I get to sneak around. First I'll sneak off our spaceship. I'll sneak over to their ice cave and gather up all those power orbs in my collector's bag.

FRIEND 2: Great! But how will we save the princess?

FRIEND 3: I have an idea! Since I'm a runner, I'll run off to the ice castle. The clones will never see me because they're standing guard right here. I'll rescue the princess and bring her back to our spaceship so we can all fly away.

FRIEND 4: But how will you get the princess out of that huge frozen block of ice she's locked inside?

FRIEND 1: I know! You can use this ice ray laser I collected on Level 1. It will melt the ice.

FRIEND 2: Perfect! Then we can all escape together.

FRIEND 1: Great idea. Let's go!

NARRATOR: The power orbs were collected from the ice cave. The clones never saw the thief. The princess was saved from the ice castle. Soon everyone was safe inside the spaceship.

FRIEND 1: The power orbs melted the ice from around our spaceship's engine and rocket boosters.

FRIEND 4: Our spaceship is free. Now we'll use those power orbs to zoom across this board and try to win this game once and for all.

CATASTROPHIC
CLONES: Stop! Stop! You've already covered 42 percent of the board. You were supposed to be frozen in time for longer than a thousand freezing years. Where did you get those power orbs?

FRIEND 2: Keep going! Now we've flown through 63 percent of the board.

FRIEND 3: Keep going! Now we've flown through 88 percent of the board. Good-bye, clones!

FRIEND 4: We did it! We flew through 100 percent of the board! We won the game!

FRIEND 1: Wow! That was the best video game ever! Do you want to play again?

TATUMN: Listen, I don't know what happened, but I've been frozen in a block of ice ever since school let out today. I didn't even have a chance to finish my homework.

FRIEND 2: But how did you get in the ice castle?

TATUMN: Don't ask me! I was just walking home from school when suddenly . . . whoosh! There I was, frozen in a block of ice inside that freezing ice castle.

FRIEND 3: But that is so strange. We hadn't even opened the video game box yet.

TATUMN: I don't know about you, but that's one game I don't ever want to play again, no matter what. Count me out. I'm going home to finish my math.

FRIENDS 1, 2, 3, AND 4: Math? We didn't know we had math homework. What is it?

TATUMN: Percents. The bonus question is to write a story using percents. What story are you going to write about?

FRIENDS 1, 2, 3, AND 4: The Out of This World Video Game!

POSSIBLE EXTENSIONS

1. Dots, Squares, and Percentages. Divide students into pairs. Have each pair draw one grid of 11 by 11 dots on a piece of paper. Blank paper may be used, but lined paper or graph paper might make this easier. The first player draws a line and connects two dots next to each other. The second player then draws a line and connects two dots. If a player completes a square, he or she writes her initial in that square and takes another turn. When all the squares have been completed on the grid, players calculate the percentage of squares they each completed. The player with the highest percent of squares wins the game.

2. Fractions, Decimals, and Percents Card Game. Use blank index cards to create a deck of cards representing various fractions, decimals, and percents, based on the skill level you are teaching. For instance, you may make the following cards (one number per card): 3/5, .23, 18%.

    Divide the cards evenly between two players. Play according to the rules of the card game War. Each player turns over one card. Both players then use paper and pencils to determine which card has the greatest value. The player with the larger number gets both cards. These cards are added to the bottom of the winner's deck.

    If players turn over two cards that have equal value, both players then turn over three more of their own cards and compare the third ones. The player with the larger number on this last card gets all the cards from that turn to add to the bottom of his or her deck.

    The player who wins all the cards or who has the most cards by the end of the session wins the game.

3. Fill in the Grid. Use blank index cards to create a deck of cards representing various fractions, decimals, and percents, based on the skill level you are teaching. For instance, you may make the following cards (one number per card): 3/5, .23, 18%.

    Two to four players may play this game. Make more cards if more players participate. Each player needs a 10-by-10 grid, pencil or crayon, and scrap paper. The dealer shuffles the cards and deals three cards to each player to hold in his or her "hand." The rest of the deck is placed facedown in the "draw pile."

    To play the game, the first player takes one card from the draw pile. She may select that card or a card from her original hand to "play." Play consists of placing a card face-up in a "discard pile" and shading that percent of squares on her grid with a pencil or crayon.

    Play continues with the next player choosing to take one card from the draw pile *or* the discard pile. (The same card from the discard pile may only be used two times. The second time it is discarded, it may not be chosen again. This prevents every player choosing to use the same card over and over again.) The second player should then choose which card to place face-up in the discard pile and shade in that percent of squares on his grid.

    Play continues as each new player draws and discards another card. Each time, the player shades in the percent of added squares on his grid. For instance, if a player discards the card ".2", she will shade in 20 squares on her grid. For the next turn, if she discards the card 14%, she will shade in 14 more squares on her grid for a total of 34 squares.

    The first player to shade in all the squares on his grid wins the game. Cards may be re-shuffled from the discard pile and placed in the draw pile as needed.

4. Ice Cream Social. Gather data regarding the number of students who like each different topping or flavor at a local ice cream store. Then together calculate the percentage of students who like each topping or flavor.

To extend this activity, divide the class into small groups and gather data within each group. Have students calculate the percentage of classmates who like each topping or flavor within each small group. Record the data on a pie chart, graph, map, or other chart according to the skill level you are studying.

Host an ice cream social in your classroom with the toppings or flavors that the highest percentage of students like best.

Invite students to write in math journals about what they learned during this math lesson. Provide art supplies for them to make a poster explaining the math concept while comparing their favorite toppings or flavors with the results for the rest of the class.

CHAPTER **14**

Scavenger Hunt (Probability)

STAGING: Seat the three campers in the center of the stage. The narrator may be seated at the far left front of the stage. The cabin leader should sit just behind the narrator but next to the campers. Both the girls' team and the boys' team may sit in separate groups toward the right side of the stage.

CHARACTERS

Narrator	Girls' Team
Cabin Leader	Boys' Team
Campers 1, 2, and 3	

	Camper 1	Camper 2	Camper 3	Girls' Team
Cabin	X	X	X	X X X X
Leader				
X				Boys' Team
				X X X X
Narrator				
X				

Scavenger Hunt

NARRATOR: It was the first day at Adventure Camp. The new campers enjoyed a great meal of hamburgers and French fries. Then they sat around the campfire. It was dark and almost time for bed.

CABIN LEADER: Welcome to Adventure Camp, where every day is an adventure! We've got hiking, rock climbing, a ropes course, water skiing, and lots and lots of bears. You'll love it here! Except for the bears. You have to watch out for the bears.

CAMPER 2: If every day is an adventure, do you have an adventure for today? We've been here all day and all we got to do is eat, find our cabin, and meet here.

CABIN LEADER: Of course we have an adventure for today! We're going to end this very first day with a scavenger hunt. It's kind of like a treasure hunt, only instead of a map, I give you a list of items to find. The first team to find all three items on their list and bring them back to me is the winner. And the winner gets to skip dishwashing duty tomorrow.

CAMPERS 1, 2, AND 3: Let's be on the same team!

GIRLS' TEAM: We'll be on a team together, too, so we can help protect ourselves from all those bears.

BOYS' TEAM: We predict we'll be on the *winning* team. Nobody can find things for the scavenger hunt as fast as we'll be able to find them!

CABIN LEADER: Okay. We've got three teams. Here are your lists. Read them carefully. There's just one important rule you have to follow. It's nighttime now, and every single team has to search for everything in the dark by the light of the moon. No lights on in the cabins. And no flashlights!

CAMPER 3: You're kidding, right?

CABIN LEADER: Not at all! If I find anyone using any kind of lights, you'll be disqualified from the scavenger hunt. And remember, the first team to find everything on your list is the winner. Starting now!

CAMPER 1: This is going to be tough. But I guess it's tough for everyone. Let's get started looking right away so we don't waste any time. What's the first item on our list?

CAMPER 2: The list says we have to find one black sock. The best thing will be to start looking in our own cabins, especially in our own suitcases. It's not going to be easy looking in the dark, though.

CAMPER 1: Okay, did anyone here bring any black socks in their suitcase? It's going to have to be one of you, because I didn't bring any black socks at all. I only packed white socks.

CAMPER 2: I only brought white socks along for the entire week, too, so we don't need to look through the stuff in my suitcase.

CAMPER 3: Let me think. Now I remember. I brought four black socks and four white socks. I brought two pairs of each kind. I wanted a variety.

CAMPER 1: Let's start in your cabin, then.

NARRATOR: The three friends hiked through the moonlight down a trail to Cabin 8. They went inside.

CAMPER 3: It's pretty dark in here, but here's my suitcase, and here are my eight socks. It's too dark, though, to tell which socks are black and which socks are white. Do either of you have any ideas about what we should do to continue our search?

CAMPER 2: If we just randomly pick out any sock, what is the probability that we'll get one black sock?

CAMPER 3: First let's figure out the outcome. Since there are eight socks, there are eight possible outcomes for picking one black sock. Right?

CAMPER 1: Right. But how do we know which one we're most likely to pick, a black one or a white one?

CAMPER 2: It's equally likely that we'll randomly pick either a white sock or a black sock as our first choice. Four of the eight socks are black, so the probability of picking a black sock is 4/8.

CAMPER 1: That's half. So if we pick half the socks, I predict we'll get a black one.

CAMPER 3: But we might pick all four white ones! So just to be certain of the outcome since we can't see them, let's pick one more sock than half.

CAMPER 2: Great idea! If we pick five socks, it's absolutely guaranteed that we'll have at least one black one in the bunch we take back to show the cabin leader.

CAMPER 1: I'm just glad we don't have to find one purple sock.

CAMPER 3: That would have been impossible for us to find in our own suitcases.

NARRATOR: The three friends picked five socks out of the suitcase. Then they headed out into the dark in search of the next item on their list. They passed the Girls' Team on the trail.

GIRLS' TEAM: Have you had any luck finding anything on your list for the scavenger hunt so far?

CAMPER 3: Yes! We're confident that we have one black sock even though we can't see it.

GIRLS' TEAM: That's funny. The first item on our list is one *purple* sock. Every team must have been given a different list.

CAMPER 1: The next thing on our list is one red marble. Do you have to find any marbles in the dark tonight?

GIRLS' TEAM: No. We have to go to our cabin, search through our suitcases, and find a brown hairbrush.

CAMPER 1: Do you have any idea where we might locate a red marble?

GIRLS' TEAM: There's a jar of marbles in the crafts cabin on the top shelf in the back of the room. The jar has six red marbles, one green marble, and one blue marble.

CAMPER 1: Thanks! We'll go look for it. Do you need any help looking around for a brown hairbrush?

GIRLS' TEAM:	Not at all. Everyone on our team brought one, so we're certain to find one in the first suitcase we look at.
CAMPER 3:	Have you seen any bears yet roaming around along the trails or hiding behind the trees?
GIRLS' TEAM:	No! And we don't want to!
NARRATOR:	The three friends hiked down the trail and headed toward the crafts cabin. They passed the Boys' Team.
BOYS' TEAM:	You don't plan on going inside the crafts cabin right now, do you?
CAMPER 3:	That's exactly where we're going. Why do you want to know?
BOYS' TEAM:	We just came from the crafts cabin, and there's a big bear prowling around there. We'd stay far away from the crafts cabin if we were you.
CAMPER 1:	But where else are we going to look if we want to find one red marble? That's next on our list for the scavenger hunt.
BOYS' TEAM:	Do you have to find marbles? Our list doesn't have any marbles of any color written on it for us to find.
CAMPER 2:	We just talked with the Girls' Team, and it looks like every team has a different list in this scavenger hunt.
CAMPER 3:	If you didn't have to find any marbles for the scavenger hunt, what were you doing in the crafts cabin?
BOYS' TEAM:	We had to find one yellow crayon. We knew the crafts cabin has boxes of crayons. It was the logical place for us to look.
CAMPER 1:	How did you find one yellow crayon in the dark? That must have been a very difficult item to find.
BOYS' TEAM:	It wasn't easy. We knew that one box of crayons has 16 crayons and only one of them is yellow.
CAMPER 2:	There are 16 different possible outcomes! The probability of your getting one yellow crayon is only one out of 16 tries!

119

BOYS' TEAM: That's right. We ended up taking a whole box of crayons. That way we're sure to have the yellow one we need to win the scavenger hunt.

CAMPER 1: Good idea. But we better get going and head to the crafts cabin now, or we'll run out of time.

BOYS' TEAM: Like we said earlier, we'd stay away from the crafts cabin if we were you. There's a big bear prowling around there. It could be dangerous, but do what you want.

NARRATOR: The three friends continued on their way to the crafts cabin. They kept looking and listening for bears. It was hard to see, however, in the moonlight. Finally they got to the crafts cabin and went inside.

CAMPER 1: Do you really think it's safe to be here inside the crafts cabin?

CAMPER 3: I'm not so sure the Boys' Team was telling us the truth. After all, *they* just went to the crafts cabin, and they didn't seem too scared of any bears themselves.

CAMPER 2: You're right! How could they have found the box of crayons in the dark if there was a bear? I think there's a great probability that they made up that whole story about bears.

CAMPER 1: I sure hope you're right. It's really very dark inside here. Has anyone found the marble jar yet?

CAMPER 3: It's right here. What's the probability of choosing one red marble out of this jar in the dark?

CAMPER 2: The Girls' Team said there are six red marbles, one green marble, and one blue marble. That's a total of eight marbles, so there are eight possible outcomes if we make one random choice.

CAMPER 1: Yes, there are a total of eight marbles in the jar, and six of them are red.

CAMPER 2: That means the probability of selecting one red marble is 6/8. Or 3/4.

120

CAMPER 3: That's pretty good! We've got a great chance of picking the red one in the dark out of the entire jar of marbles. Since there is only one blue marble, one green marble, and all the rest are red, we should just choose three marbles.

CAMPER 1: That way we'll be certain to have at least one red marble to take back.

NARRATOR: They picked three marbles randomly out of the jar and put the jar back on the shelf. Just then the three friends heard a low growl.

CAMPER 1: Did you hear that? I think I heard a bear! It sounded like there's one right here inside the crafts cabin with us!

CAMPER 3: I think it's just the Boys' Team trying to scare us because they want us to lose the scavenger hunt.

CAMPER 2: Hey, you! You can't scare us! We know you're not really a bear! You'll have to pretend better than that if you want to scare us away from finding a red marble here in the crafts cabin.

NARRATOR: They heard a growl again, and it was even louder this time. Then they heard a thump and a bump.

CAMPER 1: I don't know if it's a bear or not, but let's get out of here.

CAMPER 3: Oh, there's nothing to worry about. But okay, let's go. We got our red marble.

NARRATOR: The three friends walked out of the crafts cabin and headed down the trail.

CAMPER 3: What's the last item on our list that we're required to get if we want to win the scavenger hunt?

CAMPER 2: I don't know. It's too dark to read the lettering on the list our cabin leader gave us, even out here in the moonlight.

CAMPER 1: Maybe if we go back to the campfire, we can read it there and then go look. Wait! Did you hear that? I heard another growl behind us. It sounds like the bear we heard in the crafts cabin is following us.

CAMPER 3:	I bet it's the Boys' Team still trying to scare us away from finishing the scavenger hunt.
CAMPER 2:	We're not afraid of you guys, so why don't you just go back to looking for the stuff on your list and leave us alone!
CAMPER 1:	Let's hurry and get to the campfire. The Boys' Team is trying to scare us so we can't win. If we read the last thing on our list, maybe we can find it fast and be the winners.
NARRATOR:	The three friends ran down the rest of the trail in the darkness, back to the campfire.
CABIN LEADER:	Welcome back, campers! Did you have an exciting adventure collecting all three items on your list? But wait! Here come the Girls' Team and the Boys' Team, too!
GIRLS' TEAM:	Help! Help! A big bear is chasing us through the woods!
BOYS' TEAM:	Aaaaah! A big bear is chasing us through the woods, too!
CAMPER 1:	We only found two items on our list. We came back here to read what the third one is.
CAMPER 2:	Why, look here! The third item on our scavenger hunt is to find a bear!
GIRLS' AND BOYS' TEAMS:	That's our last item, too!
CABIN LEADER:	Well, did you each find a bear?
CAMPER 1:	We didn't. The Boys Team tried to scare us and tell us there was a bear at the crafts cabin. Then they growled and made it sound like there was a bear.
BOYS' TEAM:	That wasn't us. There really was a bear. We tried to warn you when we saw you on the trail, but you wouldn't listen to anything we told you.
NARRATOR:	Suddenly, three great big bears ran growling up to the campfire.
CAMPER 1:	And here comes that bear after us now!

GIRLS' TEAM:	There's the bear that was chasing us, too! We recognize the way it slouches when it runs.
BOYS' TEAM:	And there's the bear that was chasing us! We recognize his long black snout and little ears.
CABIN LEADER:	Congratulations! You all won! Nobody has to do dishwashing duty tomorrow because it's a three-way tie.
CAMPER 2:	The probability of that happening is highly unlikely.
CABIN LEADER:	Hurry! Now that you're all tied as the winners of the scavenger hunt, everyone should run back to your cabins! Now!
BOYS' TEAM:	But now the bears are busy eating our marshmallows that we were going to toast.
GIRLS' TEAM:	While they're busy, we better get back to our cabins and shut the doors. We don't want those bears to follow us inside.
CABIN LEADER:	See you tomorrow morning here at Adventure Camp! This is the camp where every day is filled with adventure, and every night is filled with bears.

POSSIBLE EXTENSIONS

1. Show the class several spinners with two or three colors. Discuss the possible outcomes for each spinner and the probability that the spinner will land on a certain color. Provide students with crayons or markers along with tagboard or file folders and invite them to design one or more spinners of their own. Use paper clips and pencils for the spinners.

   When students are finished, ask them to share the possible outcomes and probability of their spinners landing on certain colors. As an extra bonus, have students each develop a game to play with their spinners. Divide the class into small groups and allow time for students to play each other's games. When they're done, instruct students to write in their journals about the games they played.

2. Provide each student with a lunch-sized brown paper bag, 24 blank index cards, and crayons and markers. Instruct students to draw shapes or objects on their cards, one per card. For instance, one student might draw six black socks, six red socks, six green socks, and six purple socks. Have each student write down predictions about what they think will be the probability of picking each type of card.

   Divide students into pairs and have them pick cards randomly from their bags without looking. Each time they should return their cards back to the bag. Instruct them to tally their results on a chart. When they're finished, compare their results with their original predictions.

3. Visit these Web sites for probability worksheets and activities:

   - www.abcteach.com/directory/middle_school/math/data_analysis_probability/

   - http://msteacher.org/epubs/math/math6/lessons.aspx

   - www.shodor.org/interactivate/activities/

4. Design a bulletin board with a large working spinner in the center of the board. Create a list of vocabulary words on the board, such as *probability*, *outcome*, *certain*, *likely*, *unlikely*, and *impossible*. Ask students to each choose one or more words to demonstrate with a definition, a chart, a word problem, or a mathematical equation, using the spinner as their reference. For instance, if the spinner is divided into three equal regions of red, yellow, and blue, a student could write: "It is impossible for the arrow of the spinner to land on green." Have students check each other's work, then write or draw their "definitions" on matching pieces of paper to mount on the board. Group similar definitions together on the board. For extended learning, change the spinner several times throughout the unit and repeat the activity.

5. Yahtzee Probability. Invite small groups of students to play a game of Yahtzee while learning more about probability. According to their skill level, have students make predictions and tally the results of various dice combinations that they are trying to score while they are playing the game.

CHAPTER 15

I Spy Up in the Sky (Graphing on a Coordinate Plane)

STAGING: Seat the narrator at the front right of the stage. The four sailors may be seated in the center of the stage, with the crew standing or seated behind them. The captain should be sitting near the front left of the stage.

CHARACTERS

Narrator	Crew
Captain of the *Pinta*	Sailors 1, 2, 3, and 4

```
                          Crew
                     X      X      X
                        X      X


        Sailor 1      Sailor 2      Sailor 3      Sailor 4
           X             X             X             X

     Captain                                              Narrator
       X                                                     X
```

I Spy Up in the Sky

NARRATOR: In the early fall of 1492, a daring expedition took place. Christopher Columbus set sail from Spain across the Atlantic Ocean. He believed he could reach Asia sailing west across the sea. Columbus was captain of the *Santa María*. Another captain sailed on the *Niña*. A third captain sailed on board the *Pinta*.

CAPTAIN OF THE PINTA: All right, crew! Listen up! It's time for the night watch, so who is on duty this week?

SAILORS 1, 2, 3, AND 4: We are.

CAPTAIN OF THE PINTA: Then get to your stations. Watch the cannons in case we're attacked. The rest of the crew, go below deck and turn in to bed.

CREW: Wait! We don't want to spend another night sailing west. We want to turn around and sail for home. We declare mutiny!

SAILOR 1: I agree. We've been sailing west now for a month. Nobody has ever sailed this far west.

CREW: Columbus is crazy, because he says the world is round, but we believe it is flat like a pancake. Just look at how the compass isn't pointing true north any more. Something's wrong here.

SAILOR 3: We're going to fall off the earth for certain if we keep sailing west. I'm with the rest of the crew. I want to turn around and sail back home to Spain.

CAPTAIN OF THE PINTA: What do the rest of you sailors say? Are you willing to sail west any more, or do you want to turn around?

CREW: I think Columbus is hiding something from us. I heard that he keeps two journals. One journal is a secret journal. It has the real distance we're traveling.

SAILOR 4: The other journal is the one he shows us. The records he's written down say we haven't really sailed very far west yet.

CAPTAIN OF THE
PINTA: I've heard that, too. And the winds are blowing strong and steady toward the west. How will we ever sail back home against the wind?

CREW: I say we organize a rebellion tonight against Columbus! We'll climb aboard his ship and force him to turn the fleet around.

CAPTAIN OF THE
PINTA: Not so fast. Let's give Columbus one last chance before we approve this. If we don't reach land in three days, we all turn around and sail home.

CREW: All right. But that's his last opportunity to prove his theory is right that we'll reach Asia by sailing west. If we don't reach land in three days, we're going home.

NARRATOR: The captain and crew headed down below deck, and soon they were fast asleep in their hammocks. Four sailors kept watch all during the long, long night.

SAILOR 1: I'm tired. I can hardly stay awake. I wish there was something to look at, but there's not. It's too dark to see anything.

SAILOR 2: It's not dark if you look up at the sky where all the millions of stars are shining.

SAILOR 3: I'm having a hard time staying awake, too. Does anybody know a game we could play in the dark?

SAILOR 4: I know what we can do while the fleet is sailing along! Let's play a game I used to play a long time ago. It's called I Spy Up in the Sky.

SAILOR 1: That sounds like fun! I'll try anything to stay awake. I don't want to fall asleep on my watch. Our ship might fall off the edge of the world.

SAILOR 2: How do we play the game? Are the rules very difficult?

SAILOR 4: First, everyone needs a piece of graph paper and a feather pen with ink. Here, I have some in my knapsack. We can all share.

SAILOR 3: Thanks. Now that we have what we need to get started, what do the rules say to do next?

SAILOR 4: I look up in the sky and choose one constellation. You have to guess which constellation I've chosen. I'll give you clues. The first person to guess correctly gets to pick the next constellation.

SAILOR 1: But what are we going to do with the graph paper and pen that you gave us?

SAILOR 4: You are going to graph the map of the group of major stars in my constellation.

SAILOR 2: Should we draw the x-axis and the y-axis on our graph first?

SAILOR 4: Yes. Now let's go ahead and start. My constellation has five major stars. Draw these points on your graph: (1,6), (2,5), (1,3), (–2,5), and (0,–1).

SAILOR 2: I know which one this is! This is the herdsman!

SAILOR 4: You're right! Now it's your turn. Pick a constellation and tell us where to plot the stars on our graph.

SAILOR 2: My constellation has five major stars, too. Find these points: (1,1), (–1,–1), (4,2), (3,–2), (–5,3).

SAILOR 3: I got it this time. This group of stars is called the queen, right?

SAILOR 2: You're right. Now it's your turn to pick a constellation.

SAILOR 3: I'll pick my favorite one. It has seven stars. Get ready to plot these points on your graph: (–1,6), (–2,–4), (0,1), (1,2), (2,3), (3,5), (4,–4).

SAILOR 1: I got it! I got it! This is the hunter! I knew it was your favorite star. You look for it every night. Now it's my turn to choose, so I'll pick my favorite, too.

NARRATOR: The sailors played the game all through the night while the fleet sailed together silently on toward the west. They played it the next night, too.

128

SAILOR 4: This time, let's play the game a little differently. This time I'll tell you which constellation I picked. Then you have to find the stars in the sky and plot them on your graph. The first one who gets the correct ordered pairs first gets the next turn.

SAILOR 3: Okay. This sounds like a fun way to play I Spy Up in the Sky, too. Which group of stars will you pick first tonight?

SAILOR 4: How about Hercules? Do any of you know where its position is up in the sky?

SAILOR 1: I see it. It has seven major stars. Give me a minute to draw its stars on my paper. There. The points on my graph are: (1,3), (2,1), (3,3), (3,0), (–2,-4), (0,–1), (4,–2).

SAILOR 2: You really spotted it quickly! Now it's your turn.

SAILOR 1: For my turn tonight, I pick the image of the swan. It has six stars. I like how it appears to be flying through the night sky. Does anyone see it?

SAILOR 3: I do! This is another one of my favorites. It reminds me of the beautiful swans and other birds back home.

SAILOR 1: Do you want to plot the stars on your graph and then tell us the points where you drew them?

SAILOR 3: Of course! The points are: (–1,1), (–2,–2), (0,0), (2,2), (2,–1), (4,–2).

NARRATOR: The sailors continued to play the game on through the long hours of the night. Soon the stars faded from the sky, the sun rose up over the eastern horizon, and it was morning once more.

SAILOR 1: The stars aren't shining any more. We can't play the game again until it gets dark again tonight. I really like it, though. It helps me stay awake! Our ship isn't going to fall off the edge of the world on my watch.

SAILOR 2: Look! What's that I see out there in the water floating along in the ocean waves? It looks like some kind of board!

SAILOR 3: How can there be a board in the ocean? A board has to be made by a person. Don't you mean a piece of driftwood? We see driftwood floating along in the water all the time.

SAILOR 4: No, it's a board. I see it now, too! If there's a board floating in the waves, it means we must be near civilization.

SAILOR 1: Go get the captain! And wake up the crew. We need to tell them about what we've discovered while they've been asleep.

NARRATOR: The captain and crew jumped out of their hammocks and came running up on deck.

CAPTAIN OF THE PINTA: What's all this shouting about? What have you found?

SAILOR 2: We found a board floating past our ship in the water. Here! We fished it out of the water so everyone could examine it.

CREW: You can tell by the way it's cut and shaped that someone with tools made that board. It's not just a piece of ordinary driftwood like what we've seen floating past now and then since leaving Spain. Do you think we're near land and some kind of civilized people?

CAPTAIN OF THE PINTA: I don't know. This is very strange. Do you think Columbus was right? The world really might be round, and we could be sailing straight to Asia.

NARRATOR: All that day, the sailors and crew kept an eye on the ocean for more discoveries as the fleet continued to sail.

SAILOR 1: Look! Look there! I think I see a long brown pole floating past our ship on the other side.

SAILOR 4: And I see a stick floating by. That's not an ordinary stick, either. This stick was made by tools just like the board was.

CAPTAIN OF THE PINTA: Hurry, crew! Get those things out of the water before it gets too dark to see them.

NARRATOR:	The sailors pulled the stick and the pole out of the water. They examined them closely. They decided that both items were fashioned out of wood by people who used tools to make them. Soon it was night again.
CAPTAIN OF THE *PINTA*:	Whose turn is it on watch tonight?
SAILORS 1, 2, 3, AND 4:	It's still our turn.
CREW:	We want to stay up, too, and keep several lookouts stationed in the dark on various parts of the ship. Do you think we might see land?
CAPTAIN OF THE *PINTA*:	I can't say. But anyone who wants to stay up tonight may. After all, this is the last night we're sailing west. If we don't reach land by morning, we will turn around and sail straight back home.
NARRATOR:	All through the long, long hours of the night, the sailors watched and waited. Everyone was tense and expectant. Finally, one sailor gave a shout.
SAILOR 3:	Land! Land ho! I see land straight ahead!
NARRATOR:	The long voyage was soon to be over. The sailors found land, but it was not the land Columbus thought it was. They thought it was Asia. It wasn't until much later that people learned this was a continent they had never seen before. They had landed in America.

POSSIBLE EXTENSIONS

1. Distribute graph paper to students and have them plot the constellations with the coordinates listed in the play, each constellation on its own coordinate plane. Have them study a constellation chart and plot several of their choices. As an added extension, invite them to invent their own constellations to plot on a graph, such as the Chair, the Penguin, the Polar Bear, or the Airplane. Constellation charts may be found in the following book or Web sites:

    –   *The Night Sky: An Introduction to Prominent Stars and Constellations* by James Kavanagh

    –   www.sorosy.com/picture.phtml?fileid=385&noprint=0

    –   http://mail.colonial.net/~hkaiter/zodiacconstellations.html

    –   http://space.about.com/od/backyardscience/ss/constellcannist.htm:

    –   Constellation in a Canister: Click on the link to "View Pattern" under "What you need."

2. Divide students into pairs to play a paper and pencil game of Water Balloon Toss. Provide graph paper and instruct students to each draw a coordinate plane with an x-axis labeled from −10 to 10 and a y-axis labeled from −10 to 10.

    Have each player randomly draw the following "people" on the coordinate plane: one child (length of two consecutive ordered pairs), three teens (each one the length of three consecutive ordered pairs) and two adults (each one the length of four consecutive ordered pairs). Each person is represented by two, three, or four consecutive points on the plane.

    Players try to find each other's "people" and tag them with a "water balloon" by taking turns calling out ordered pairs. The first player to find all the people on the other's graph wins the game.

3. Distribute graph paper and invite students to each draw a map of an amusement park on a grid according to the skill level you are teaching. When they are finished, provide art supplies for students to draw or construct a 3-dimensional model of the amusement park that corresponds with the locations of each ride or concession on the map. Completed models may be displayed on their desks. Allow time for students to walk around the room and look at each other's amusement park designs.

4. Play a game of Ordered Pairs Bingo. On a piece of typing paper, prepare a blank 5-by-5-inch grid to resemble a standard Bingo card. In the center square, write "Free Space." At the top of each column, instead of writing B-I-N-G-O, write in this order: "Quadrant I," "Quadrant II," "Axes," "Quadrant III," and "Quadrant IV." (Note: Adjust the game according to the skill level of your students.)

    Photocopy the Ordered Pairs Bingo card and distribute one to each student. On the board, overhead projector, or bulletin board, display a coordinate plane with an x-axis labeled from −10 to 10 and a y-axis labeled from −10 to 10 and with each quadrant labeled I through IV. Direct students to then randomly choose ordered pairs from each quadrant to write in the corresponding columns on their own Bingo cards until the cards are full. Under the column for Axes, students will write ordered pairs found on the x-axis or y-axis such as (1,0) or (0,−2). Have students each tear or cut a piece of red construction paper into one-inch pieces to use as markers for the board. Each player needs 25 markers.

    Provide graph paper and instruct students to each draw a coordinate plane with an x-axis labeled from −10 to 10 and a y-axis labeled from −10 to 10.

    Play the game according to the rules for regular Bingo. Call out different ordered pairs from the axes or different quadrants, such as (3,6), (–2, 5), (0,3) and (2,1). Instruct students to also plot each point on their grids if they have that ordered pair on their Bingo boards. Mark the points you call on a separate coordinate plane of your own to check students' work. The winner is the first player (or players) to complete a predetermined pattern on his or her (or their) board(s), such as a line (either vertical, horizontal, or diagonal) or a full house (all the squares are covered). New coordinate planes will need to be drawn each time the game is played.

5.   Ask students to create a treasure map on a coordinate plane. Then have them write directions for walking from point to point in order to locate the treasure. When they are finished, have a volunteer read his or her instructions to the class while another student draws the corresponding points on a coordinate plane on the overhead projector or board. Discuss results and repeat this activity with various volunteers.

About the Authors

JEFF SANDERS has taught at Fairmont Elementary School in Yorba Linda, California, for most of his 28-year career as an elementary classroom teacher. Both a National Blue Ribbon School as well as a California Distinguished School, Fairmont Elementary School has been like a second home to Jeff. He truly feels connected to the staff as well as students and their parents as part of his extended family. His classroom environment supports his philosophy that students learn better while having fun and experiencing important ingredients of childhood. Jeff's students learn how to saw, drill, and sand wood. Accompanied by his guitar, they sing songs and study composers ranging from Handel to Elvis. Each spring parents and siblings are invited to visit for Jeff's California Gold Rush unit, for which the classroom is transformed into a fully functioning gold-mining town.

NANCY I. SANDERS is the best-selling author of more than 75 books. Her picture book, *D Is for Drinking Gourd: An African American Alphabet* (2007) is a winner of the 2007 NAPPA Honors book award as well as other awards and is illustrated by Caldecott Honor award-winning illustrator E. B. Lewis. Her essential book for writers, *Yes! You Can Learn How to Write Children's Books, Get Them Published, and Build a Successful Writing Career*, is the award-winning finalist of the National Best Books 2009 Awards. One of Nancy's newest books is the ground-breaking *America's Black Founders: Revolutionary Heroes and Early Leaders with 21 Activities* (For Kids series, 2010). Her Web site may be found at www.nancyisanders.com and her blog at www.nancyisanders.wordpress.com. At both places teachers may find a selection of classroom resources, and students will find opportunities to get a behind-the-scenes glimpse into the life of a published author.

This is Jeff and Nancy's fifth book together as a teacher/author and husband/wife team. They have also cowritten *Readers Theatre for African American History* (Teacher Ideas Press, 2008).